2009 Poetry Co

I have a
dream 2009

Words to change the world

Martin Luther King

John Lennon

Essex

Edited by Vivien Linton

First published in Great Britain in 2009 by:

 Young**Writers**

Young Writers
Remus House
Coltsfoot Drive
Peterborough
PE2 9JX
Telephone: 01733 890066
Website: www.youngwriters.co.uk

Foreword

'I Have a Dream 2009' is a series of poetry collections written by 11 to 18-year-olds from schools and colleges across the UK and overseas. Pupils were invited to send us their poems using the theme 'I Have a Dream'. Selected entries range from dreams they've experienced to childhood fantasies of stardom and wealth, through inspirational poems of their dreams for a better future and of people who have influenced and inspired their lives.

The series is a snapshot of who and what inspires, influences and enthuses young adults of today. It shows an insight into their hopes, dreams and aspirations of the future and displays how their dreams are an escape from the pressures of today's modern life. Young Writers are proud to present this anthology, which is truly inspired and sure to be an inspiration to all who read it.

Contents

Chelmsford College

Christian Piggott (18)............................ 1

Clacton County High School

Rebecca Johnson (12) 2
Molly Aldis (12) 3
Tom Moodey (13)................................... 4
Amber Bellinger (11) 5
Emilie Flack (12).................................... 6

Honywood Community Science School

Oliver Stephens (14)............................... 7
Amy McFadden (12) 8
Robbie Naylor (11)................................. 9
Flora Buckley (12) 10
Ellen McIntosh (11)...............................11
Victoria Nash (14) 12
Isaac Kean (14) 13
Lucy Claisse (12) 14
Katie Chaplin (11) 15

St Peter's High School, Burnham-on-Crouch

Kristina Olliffe (12)............................... 15
Jordan Spinks (12) 17
Ryan Goff (11) 17
Tom Connelly (14) 18
Emma Leigh Boyce (11) 19
Hannah Harden (13)............................. 20
Jade McGachan (14)............................ 21
Shannon Richards (12)........................ 22
Katie Amey (13) 23
Joe Walker (12) 23
Joe Howard (11) 24
Demi Lee Ellis...................................... 24
Roseannaha Newman-Clark (12).......... 25
Leah Anstey (13) 25
Jamie Candler (11) 26
Tom Langmead (12) 26
Curtis (12).. 27

Abigail Rolfe (13).................................. 27
Alice Tavinor (12)................................. 28
Madison Butler (12) 29
Megan MacLaine (13)........................... 29
Kira Anderson (11) 30
Daniel Bill (12) 30
Victoria Peterson (12)........................... 31
Sophie Bache (14)................................ 31
Lara Stewart (11) 32
Reggie Powell (13) 32
Katie Whitley (12) 33
Nealie Deacon (12)............................... 33
Georgina Lowe (12).............................. 34
Sarah Murfitt (12)................................ 34
Laura Broughton (12) 35
Bradley Ramsey (11) 35
Lauren Poyntz (11) 36
Demi Searles (11)................................. 36
Ella Dennerley (12).............................. 37
Louise Pierpoint (12) 37
Nadine Smith (12)................................ 38
Sam Barr (12)...................................... 38
Megan Plumb (12)................................ 39
Oliver Cridland (12) 39
Angel Di-Capite (11) 40
Shannon Bullen (12)............................. 40
David Boyd (12)................................... 41
Kenny Harber (11) 41
William Francis (13).............................. 42
Sophie-Leigh Royce (11) 42
James Sebborn (12).............................. 43
Darrielle Hunt (11) 43
Chloe Shaw (11).................................. 44
Jamie Good (11).................................. 44
Clare Thurtle (12) 45
Samuel Connelly (11) 45
Brandon Hunt (13)............................... 46
Alex Garrett (12)................................. 46
Cecily Cole (13)................................... 47
Matthew Newbury (13) 47
Alison Aspinall (12).............................. 48

Jack Finch (13) 48
Ryan Davies (12) 49
Megan Anderton (13) 49
Victoria Ponder (12) 50
Samuel Park (12) 50
Lily Paciuszko (13) 51
Harry Edwards (14) 51
Ryanjay Culff (13) 52
Hannah Lote (13) 52
Michael Joslin (12) 53
Richard Cunningham (13) 53
Rachel Stedman (12) 54
Kirsty Simmonds (11) 54
Emily Green (12) 55
Joseph Sexton (11) 55
Craig Thorpe (13) 56
Terry Stiffell (14) 56
James Williams (13) 57
Nicholas Sutton (13) 57
Chelsea Chapman (11) 58
Amie Brown (11) 58
Sandy McEwan (12) 59
Dieter Green (13) 59
Katie Banner (14) 60
Lili Nicholls (12) 60
Rachel Mason (11) 61
Jake Gullen (11) 61
Nathan Stephen Keeble (12) 62
Kerry Van Der Marel (13) 62
Andrew Mycroft (12) 63
Holli Rolph (13) 63
Nathan Martin (13) 64
Naomi Mapes (12) 64
Alice Turfkruyer (12) 65
Lola Swallow (12) 65
Shaun Green (13) 66
Michael Hayes (12) 66
Harry Dye (11) 67
Latisha Adams (14) 67
Jade Youins-Martin (13) 68
Rebecca Tatlow (13) 68
Ben Mumford (14) 69
Jack Garwood (14) 69
Elle Mardle (11) 70
Hannah Francis (12) 70

Joe Tavinor (14) 71
Grace Gay (13) 71
Ashley Brew (14) 72
Jessica Bone (14) 72
Jake Cope (13) 73
Connor Anderson (13) 73
Oliver Brown (11) 74
Adam Woodley (11) 74
Ian Smith (12) 75
James Swinger (14) 75
Jay Sadler (12) 76
Dean Wallace (13) 76
Luke Toms (11) 76
Max Beard (12) 77
Frankie Astell (13) 77
Carrie Feagan (12) 77
Tom Calvert (13) 78
Hannah Lloyd (12) 78
John Turner (11) 78
Hollie Jenkins (11) 79
Christopher Hawkes (11) 79
Katherine Watts (13) 79
George Gilbert (12) 80
Macauley Joy (12) 80
Amy Tucker (13) 80
Amy Gates (12) 81
Martin Greene (12) 81
Anna Gilbert (12) 81
Amy McKay 12) 82
Buster Harris (11) 82
Rachel Pursey (13) 82
Alexandra Middleton (12) 83
Ted Sims (12) 83
Jordan Marciniak (11) 83
Charlie Mead (11) 84
Scott Woloszczuk (11) 84
Pierce Newton (12) 84
Toni Bacon (13) 85
Joe Groom (13) 85
Ellie Patmore (14) 85
Alfie Bailey (12) 86
Sophie Bowyer (11) 86
Brooke Bell (13) 86

Conor Youins-Martin (11) 87
Sherise Ritzka (12) 87
Frankie Gore (12) 87

The Boswells School

Tom Nash (12) 88
Danuelle Paynter (12) 89
Christopher Wright (12) 90
Georgia Rainsby (11) 91
Megan Scott (12) 92
Sam Holloway (11) 92
Charlotte Wright 93
Bradley Clarke (11) 93
Lydia Brown (11) 94
Lauren Harris (11) 95
Nicole Hadley (12) 96
Dan Tipp (11) 97
Nicola Morl (12) 98
Steffy George (11) 99
Olivia Simmons (12) 99
Shailan Gohil (12) 100
Alex Heard (12) 100
Ross Toomey (11) 101
Lucy Barker (12) 101
Eden Graham (11) 102
George Clements (11) 102
Toby Heseltine (11) 103
Abigail O'Malley (11) 103
Thelma Sengere (11) 104
Lucy Matthams (12) 104
James Bush (12) 105
Liam Bush (11) 105
Georgia Williams (11) 106

The Campion School

Cedric Percy Sam (13) 106
Miguel Naveda (12) 107
Joseph Nelson (14) 109
Taylor Triphook (12) 109
Sam Keanly (12) 110
John Burnham (12) 111
Liam Snellin (13) 112
Rory Freeman (13) 113
George Lutterodt (13) 114
Charlie Gillespie (12) 115

James Doyle (12) 116
Matthew Birtles (14) 117
Alan Sabu Mathew (13) 118
Oliver Lee (13) 119
Jack Lilley (14) 119
Fionnan Byrne-Perkins (12) 120
Taylor Magner (13) 120
Tommy O'Donnell (13) 121
Joshua Myner (13) 121

The King Edmund School

Chantelle Hurrell (13) 123
Chelsea Bush (13) 123
George Watkins (11) 124
Emily Bull (12) 125
Holly Hutcheon (13) 126
Dylan Bond (13) 126
Shina McNaught (14) 127
Daniel Ward (11) 128
Jade Mott (12) 129
Timothy South (12) 129
Michael Miller (11) 130
Ben Brower (14) 130
Jack Norman (14) 131
Sam Kershaw (13) 131
Mia Cotton (12) 132
Billy Purkiss (14) 133
Serina Shelton (11) 134
Lee Aylott (11) 134
Jasmine Zekai (11) 135
Alice Repper (12) 135
George Claydon (11) 136
Abby Hare (11) 136
Connie Harrison (14) 137
Abigail Mallard (11) 137
Sherele Lord (13) 138
Connor Miles (13) 138
Thomas Bridge (13) 139
Josh Walker (12) 139

The Sandon School

Alice White (13) 140
Eleanor Crussell (12) 141
Amy Hasler (13) 142
Rhys Emery (12) 142

Aimee Tompkins (13)........................... 143
Emma Till (13) 143
Alice Brookes (12) 144
Harry Kindell-Brown (13) 144
James Moodey (13)............................. 145
Joanne Swann (13) 145
Rachel Goddard (12)........................... 146
Ryan Mark Hart (13)............................ 146

The Poems

The Word *Different* Is An Opinion

The moon and sun are brothers
And live opposite each other
In harmony to cover
The Earth their mother
For both do love her
And don't want to see her suffer
So poured water on her head
That turned into an ocean
And set about a motion
Of commotion
A sense of devotion
Where the sun took the notion
Of sacrifice
And gave its life
So that Mother Earth would see light
And survive the fight
That rages today.

Christian Piggott (18)
Chelmsford College

1

I Have A Dream

I have a dream,
A dream to do what I want.
Believing is all it takes.
If you believe you find who you really are.

Smiling at those stars,
Those stars shining in the sky.
Makes me wonder,
Wonder what would happen if I reached my dream?

Watch me dance,
Listen to me sing.
Be jealous of who I am,
And what I'm doing for myself.

Hearing the birds – *chirp, chirp chirp*
How the way they're flying . . .
Flying like they're free.
That's what I want to be.

Seeing the empty spaces in the sky,
Makes me think.
I have an empty space,
I need to fill it, fill it with my pride.

You need to believe,
Believe in yourself.
What's your dream?
Are you going to reach it?

I have a dream,
A dream to do what I want.
Believing is all it takes.
If you believe you find who you really are.

Rebecca Johnson (12)
Clacton County High School

2

I Have A Dream

I have a dream
My dream is for the world to live in harmony,
No more knife crime or drugs
But instead all we do is love.
I have another dream,
Even as small as this . . .
I'll turn a light off everyday
I know I can do it if I just believe.
I have a dream,
It's big I know
I want to perform for the rest of my life
I'm never going to let that dream go.
I had a dream,
For racism to stop
Now there is a black president
It wasn't me who did this but I still believed.
I have a dream,
For poverty to stop
In all my hopes and dreams I wish this would happen
But I can't be sure.
I know these dreams may not happen
But I will still believe
Because I have self-confidence and pride
And know that will never leave
If I can do this please do this too
If you believe all your dreams will come true.

Molly Aldis (12)
Clacton County High School

I Have A Dream

Most people have dreams
But a lot of people don't, it seems.
They sit around all day and night,
Ill or sick, not putting up a fight.

I have big dreams,
Quite a lot, so it seems.
They include the world and my family,
Jobs shortage and poverty.

People laugh at my dreams
But I don't care, as it seems.
They are big, they are small,
Want to walk on China's Great Wall!

I have a big variety of dreams,
But some are small, as it seems.
They are hugging my mum and dad,
And playing with my brother and not getting mad.

So don't take the mick out of other people's dreams,
Or they'll take the mick out of yours, as it seems
So just remember to keep your dreams,
And you will accomplish them, as it seems!

Tom Moodey (13)
Clacton County High School

I Have A Dream

I have a dream . . .
I have a dream. An inspiration. I hope you do too.
To climb trees, to write a story, anything you can do.
Life is like a light bulb. On off, on off.
Unless you have a dream, you'll lose the plot.

Barack Obama had a dream. Look at him now.
First black president, whites had a row.
Keep going, 'Never, never, never give up'
Winston Churchill's saying. It brought us luck.
Words brought us through,
You can too, only if you tried.

I have a dream. An inspiration. I hope you do too.
To climb trees, to write a story, anything you can do.
Only you can achieve a dream, it takes courage.
Many people's dream is to get married.
They did it. You can too. Only you can rely on you.

I have a dream . . . Do you?

Amber Bellinger (11)
Clacton County High School

I Have A Dream

I have a dream. I believe anything is possible. Do you?
Without fighting and wars, would the world be a better place?
With no hope or aim, will your life go to waste?

I have a dream. I believe anything is possible. Do you?
Just go for it. What do you have to lose?
Try again or give up? You choose.

I have a dream. I believe anything is possible. Do you?
Just go for the glory, all the way to the top.
When life starts to get bad just tell it to stop.

I have a dream. I believe anything is possible? Do you?
Be ambitious and brave and you will go far.
All you need remember is reach for the stars,
I have a dream. I believe anything is possible. Do you?

Emilie Flack (12)
Clacton County High School

Hear That . . . ? (Silence)

A voice crying loud,
And crying for days now,
'Is there anybody here?
Can you get me out of here?
You're walking down a road I can't go . . .'

I'll be here by the ocean,
And my dreams fall like,
Ashes of once burning flames.
And as minutes move to hours,
I'll be desperately awaiting for you,
As I'm all alone and in the dark.

Hear the voices,
Growing day by day,
Doing nothing only makes them louder.
Feel the rebellion in the air!
Makes you scream 'Why is no one here?'

So this is me with the words on the tip of my tongue,
And staring down the barrel of a loaded gun,
As all we see turns to a darker shade of grey,
It's been a long night,
A fist fight,
With words against the silence that is now.

But I've got a bad feeling about this,
Tell you and all your friends,
The horrors you've seen,
The skin, the bones, and nervous wrecks.

So reach out,
Pull me in,
Only you can make a difference,
Bring me back home tonight
All I regret is I can't finish this alone.

You be the voice that stands up,
Stop the never-ending monologue.
Save us from a decade under the influence,
The influence of silence.

Oliver Stephens (14)
Honywood Community Science School

Will The Trees Ever Get The Chance To Speak Out?

I have a dream that one day the rainforest will be free
I have a dream that it will flourish once more,
Nobody else seems that concerned even though they are all aware,

They still come with their trucks they come with their lorries,
With their weapons of terror,
They keep on coming
They don't stop.

They don't leave till all their towers of pride have fallen,
They don't leave till they are all gone
Out of sight forever more.

Please stop and think
Or God, please have mercy on our souls,
They mean no harm, please hear their calls
Let them live in peace within,
Their dwelling, their homes with their families.

Can't you hear the distant cries
The wails of pain?
Or do you block it all out with that sinister mind?
Or are you set on your goal
Won't take your eyes off the prize?
Well let me say just one thing,
You'll regret this,
You'll see.

The rainforest can't speak out, it can't complain,
What do we do?
Nothing. Nothing at all.

Now it's time for action as the time for words has been and gone,
It's not too late to make a difference, but are these words just a dream?

Amy McFadden (12)
Honywood Community Science School

I Have A Dream

I have a dream,
To stop people being mean.

To save Africa
And to stop the Mafia.

To cure AIDS
And to free the slaves.

To save polar bears
And give us a breath of fresh air.

To stop terrorism
And to clamp down on racism.

To help a nation
By giving the kids there an education.

To stop war
And give third world countries more.

To see Robert Mugabe go out of power
And to save Zimbabwe on that hour.

To find a cure for cancer
And stop oil drilling in Alaska.

To stop world debt
There are deadlines to be met.

To go into space
And save the human race.

Life's a mystery
And I want to change history.

I have a dream
Do you?

Robbie Naylor (11)
Honywood Community Science School

I Have A Dream

I have a dream,
It's not about rainbows and butterflies,
Or glittering stars and silky skies,
No unicorns in sight,
Or rave princes with their swords of might,
You cannot hear the mermaids singing,
Or the good guys that are always winning,
No baddies chasing me, or big dragons that I can see,
No princesses with long, blonde hair,
But all these dreams, are just not fair.

My dream,
Is about children dying,
Their poor mothers weeping and crying,
The starving with no food in sight,
Who have to walk all day and all night,
Just to get some precious water,
They can't afford any goats to slaughter,
All they have is their sisters and brothers,
But their fathers and mothers,
Are long dead now.

So when you eat your dinner,
Just think of those children who are so much thinner,
When there's nothing on TV,
Jut don't think, *oh why me?*
And when you are forced to do the dishes,
Just think of those poor children's long lost wishes,
For they will never be found,
And eventually, those children won't be able to make a sound.

Flora Buckley (12)
Honywood Community Science School

Keep Dreaming!

I dream about living under the sea,
About mermaids and silver seahorses that shimmer like golden
nuggets,
About bubbles and rocks as smooth as melted butter,
About fish with a dozen rainbow scales,
I dream about living under the sea!

I dream about saving the rainforest!
About the trees green and plants glossy,
About the expressionless orang-utans,
About the flowing rivers and rippling streams,
I dream about saving the rainforest!

I dream about *chocolate!*
About the creamy sensations,
About the way it coats my tongue,
About the luxury of eating it,
I dream about *chocolate!*

I dream about saving children!
About ending famines and wars,
About stopping the bloodshed as thick as 1000 bees,
About the sadness that hangs around like a really bad odour,
I dream about saving children!

Everyone dreams,
But few do anything with them,
Dream big things,
And carry them out
Keep dreaming!

Ellen McIntosh (11)
Honywood Community Science School

11

One Dream

One dream
Could change the world;
Over generations,
Stories being told.

One dream
Could change a life,
Give inspiration
When in strife.

One dream
Gave the hero Robin Hood,
Who stole from the rich
And gave to the good.

One dream
Gave Martin Luther King
Who supported his people
But paid for his fighting.

One dream
Gave Shakespeare his name.
His plays were inspiring
And brought him his fame.

One dream
Could change the world;
Over generations
Stories being told.

Victoria Nash (14)
Honywood Community Science School

Voices Of The Silent

Down the hallways of the lost echo
The voices once held in loud resonance,
And in this crypt of blame lies only the nature
Of man, himself.
For those which were
Are not always in some great battle locked.
No, their only wish was that of the farmer,
Not of the fighter.
But is it to mourn those we knew not?
To stop what we, ourselves, are guilty of?
But, he who saves one life saves the world entire,
And those who send their hands to resolve upon them,
Only then can clear conscience be.
Conflict will always rage in some far-off land.
And ignorance will always remain
In such grace.
But, can this bitter war cease?
None will ever know.

Isaac Kean (14)
Honywood Community Science School

13

I Have A Dream

A dream can mean many things,
A wish, a sleepless night, a new toy,
It may be when a young girl sings,
Pure, strong, full of joy,
It may scare,
Terrifying, frightening, spooky,
It may show you living life with not a care,
Happiness, laughter, ever so merry,
It may take you back to when you were young,
Little, oblivious, vulnerable,
It may be like a fairy story told among,
Unreal, wonderful, impossible,
It may be magical,
Flying men, hand standing dogs, a speaking squirrel!
All these things a dream could mean,
What does it mean for you?

Lucy Claisse (12)
Honywood Community Science School

I Have A Dream

I have a dream
A determined dream.
To get into
The world I love.
I am willing to do
Whatever it takes,
Because when I grow up,
I want to make a difference,
And when I'm older,
I want to have a job I love.
It's not a phase,
Like some other dreams,
It is a real, true dream,
That I want so much.
I have a dream,
To become a fashion designer.

Katie Chaplin (11)
Honywood Community Science School

Imagine If . . . The World Was A Wonderful Place!

My dream would be to help
The hungry, the homeless, the less fortunate.
Christmas, a jolly time of year.
The homeless get nothing!

We have all the food we want, perhaps more.
The hungry starve to death with only scraps of food to eat
And a drop of water to drink.

The world would be a wonderful place
If no one lived in these conditions.
So let's help the homeless, let's help the hungry
Then the world would *definitely* be a wonderful place!

Kristina Olliffe (12)
St Peter's High School, Burnham-on-Crouch

I Have A Dream

I had a dream that I was a football player,
And played for a professional football team,
Playing in real football stadiums,
And playing for a great team,
And earning good money,
But the team I would play for is either Southend United or Arsenal FC
Because they are the best teams in the world,
Scoring screamer goals and everyone cheering me on,
And I would love to play against teams
Like Colchester or Tottenham Hotspur,
And the most exciting thing's playing against teams across other
                                                    countries,
The positions I love to play in are either striker or midfielder,
But the positions I don't like to play is goalkeeper or defender,
I think of myself as a confident player
But sometimes playing real football I am not used to.
I don't play for a football team at the moment
But when I am older I will try my best to join a football team,
One of my friends plays for Maldon football team
And plays every weekend,
I usually play football down the park or at school
With my mates most of every week,
And as it's coming up for summertime,
I will bring in my football every day,
Summer is my favourite time of year
And that's when I am always out playing football,
But it would mean everything to me
To play professional football in front of thousands of fans
And scoring goals as well,
I watch football a lot in stadiums and on TV
And I'm always thinking what it would be I like to play football
                                                    like that,
Overall this country's favourite sport is either football or rugby.
And that to other countries maybe very different,
I started football when I was very little
And over the years I have got much better,
I love all sports, but I am best at football
And I have been commented on it as well,
When football was first found, it changed the world

And is now the most popular sport in this world today, Football is preferred for a boy sport
But today girls also like it too,
I think I would love to change the way
That people think of football players today
By not moving to the teams and earning too much money,
But today football is getting very annoying for fans
To see players earning way too much money to kick around a ball,
So I do want to play for a real team
But not earning a ridiculous amount of money to play,
But in the near future I think I would like to start off my football career
Playing for Southend United,
But overall playing for a team takes a lot of training
To play professional football and before making the choice
Ask yourself, could I play football every weekend?

Jordan Spinks (12)
St Peter's High School, Burnham-on-Crouch

I Have A Dream

Imagine . . .

I have a dream that
Poverty will end,
Homeless will have
Homes,
And people won't starve.

Imagine . . .

I have a dream
That war will stop,
Terrorists will give up
And we can all live in peace.

Imagine . . .

I have a dream,
The world will not be alone,
And people will be happy forever.

Ryan Goff (11)
St Peter's High School, Burnham-on-Crouch

Imagine

Imagine there is no bullying
Everyone would get along
People are kind
And are sharing
No arguing, everyone getting along.

Imagine there's no drugs
No one wishing they could stop
People not damaging their brains
No one dying from an overdose.

Imagine there's no smoking
Helping the environment
Also helping their lungs
No one dying from smoking.

Imagine there's no underage sex
No one wishing they could go back
And change what they have done.

Imagine there's no environment hurting creations
The world would be beautiful
People helping the environment
Recycling helps
So recycle as much as possible
Help us change the world.

No one crying about people dying
It helps us all.

I'm a helpful person
There's a lot of us around
We like to help
I'm improving the land.

All of this can change the world
So please stop hurting the environment,
Yourself and others around you.

Tom Connelly (14)
St Peter's High School, Burnham-on-Crouch

I Have A Dream

I have a dream of freedom
Freedom smells like apple pie
I'm five minutes away from freedom
I can feel it from the tip of my fingers

I have a dream of freedom
I came into this world with this dream
And when I die, I will hopefully have completed it
If I have not, I'll pass this dream on
To the next heir, to the throne in my family

I have an aim,
I'm aiming to get it
This is my goal in my life
My goal will be completed, I'm sure

I have a dream
To have my kid to be free from this horrible nightmare
I can't go to sleep at night worrying about my slavery
I don't care about going to jail, for protesting for what is right
They can put me in jail, for 27 years, I would not care

I have a dream
That they will let us go free before my kids become slaves
I have a feeling they won't know
I hope, I hope
I wish, I wish
I really hope and wish

If they have a heart
They will let us go free
This is what I believe in
And I hope I'm remembered for this

Why are we the slaves, not them?
Why us?
Please help us, we beg.

Emma Leigh Boyce (11)
St Peter's High School, Burnham-on-Crouch

19

I Have A Dream

That the world
Would be a dream world,
Where all the nations
Are joined with no discrimination
And where global warming
Is no more a warning
Where our future
Is everyone's
Future . . .
I dream
That children are loved
Love is in everyone.
Everyone has hope
And hope is the world
Our dream world
Full of friendship,
Not jealousy.
Families
Not homeless
Where dreams come true,
Where Martin Luther King's dream
Is reality,
Hope, friendship, love and families.
Our life is not a dream,
But sometimes . . .
Life is not reality . . .
It's a dream.

Hannah Harden (13)
St Peter's High School, Burnham-on-Crouch

20

I Have A Dream

Gays are seen as not normal
But they are you see, because there is no such thing as normal
And anyway you can't help who you fall in love with

Don't judge by skin colour
If you're black, white or half-cast it doesn't matter
We're all the same inside

In school you have groups, different cliques
Geeks, Goths, jocks, first years and more
But don't tease; it's just a group . . . so mingle

For some people they get bullied because of their family
If their mum or dad is in prison, or not around anymore
And silly things like that

Celebrities get treated like royalty
With news reporters following them around
But some don't like it they're just like us you know

Some people don't get accepted . . . because of where they're from
Scotland, Wales, Ireland, America
It's just a country. Get over it!

And the most common is for the way people look
If you have spots, glasses, the way you dress
But please people, remember everyone has feelings

So this is my poem, this is what I have to say
Accept people for who they are and then everyone is happy
Just because someone isn't like you doesn't make them an outcast.

Jade McGachan (14)
St Peter's High School, Burnham-on-Crouch

21

Foster Care

If there was no such thing as foster care
There would be loads of people unhappy or homeless,
Maybe injured or seriously hurt.
I could have been anywhere, but thanks to some fantastic people
Who decided to take in children.
No hunger makes a change and changes someone's life.
This is my poem about foster care.

Mum, why'd you give me up?
Dad, why'd you go to prison.
I thought you guys loved me.
You ruined my whole life
I had to live with people I didn't even know.
I was walking on eggshells every single day.
I had to ask to use the refrigerator.
What to do and how to do it.
I was put in Leverton House.
Do you even care?
I was bullied by you.
You made me who I am today,
You made me just like you,
And I don't like it.
I ain't that same little girl you raised.
No one can relate to me.
My life is passing by.
You wonder why I don't want anything to do with you.
I like it here.

Shannon Richards (12)
St Peter's High School, Burnham-on-Crouch

I Had A Dream

Upside down,
Topsy turvey,
Dreams and aspirations,
The life we lead,
Reveals the truth,
Of unnatural hibernations,

To help others,
We must help ourselves,
Find right in what we do,
Put an end to poverty,
Cure the fatal,
Take the opportunities we're open to,

I believe my life's ambition,
Is making wrongs disappear,
Lay on hands to the broken hearted,
Design artificial limbs,
That in time will grow,
Replacing those before parted.

Faith can take you anywhere,
Just make sure you stay believing,
I want to help the life of others,
I *can* help the life of others,
Follow your dream,
You'll find yourself achieving.

Katie Amey (13)
St Peter's High School, Burnham-on-Crouch

My World

No guns on the street
No wars ever again
Leave police force in every district
No drugs unless prescription.

Joe Walker (12)
St Peter's High School, Burnham-on-Crouch

23

Silence

No more gangs
No more violence
Without guns
Total silence.

The days will go on
Without any deaths.

More chefs
More food
For the millions around
The world that get
Treated so rudely.

Time is short
So don't get caught
In the mess
And don't get dragged
Into Hell's nest.

No Heaven
No Hell
On one gets locked in a cell
For the crimes they do
For the years they hate.

They're not the ones
For you to slate.

Joe Howard (11)
St Peter's High School, Burnham-on-Crouch

Forgiveness

Forgiveness is something that you should do.
Forget about troubles and bad stuff that you do.
If we forgive then you should too.
I dream that we should all forgive and forget.

Demi Lee Ellis
St Peter's High School, Burnham-on-Crouch

Lost In Time

I am lost in time, I don't know what to do,
I am lost in time, I blame it all on you (Labour)
I am falling in time with love on my side
We have ruined this world with pollution and war.

Roseannaha Newman-Clark (12)
St Peter's High School, Burnham-on-Crouch

Imagine . . .

Imagine there is no war,
Then everyone will be happy,
If some countries had money,
The world would never starve.

Imagine there is no land and water,
This Earth will never survive,
So nature and animals will not be alive.

Imagine all the people,
Dying by crimes everyday,
We should stick to one another
To share our love each and every way.

You may say that I'm a dreamer,
But if the world sticks together,
The world will be a special one,
And all of us will become one.

Imagine there was no Heaven,
Why do all the people die?
Imagine if there was not a sun or a moon,
Earth would never stick together.

So people be happy for what we have got,
Some are more lucky than others,
And that should never be forgotten.

Leah Anstey (13)
St Peter's High School, Burnham-on-Crouch

Untitled

Bullied, upset, sad
Can only describe some of the feelings
That these children are feeling
Without it the whole world would *be happy*
To play and have fun in.

Jamie Candler (11)
St Peter's High School, Burnham-on-Crouch

The Life Of Our Generations

I came to the world with a beautiful start,
And I saw the love and care that I needed,
Pass by me everyday.
But as I grew older I started to see,
That not everyone had what was given to me.

It started to fill me with sorrow and shame,
And gave me the feeling that I was to blame.
But now I know what I must do,
I must save the world in a personal way,
To walk around the world and say,
That what sins we commit will scar the Earth,
And hurt the future generations straight from birth.
It is the generations that are to come,
Who feel the pain of what we've done.
I dream of a day when everyone listens,
To the cries of their unborn children,
When they feel the pain of what we've left.

We leave murder, horror, the sorrow of war,
The generations feel easily torn
But we need to leave happiness and ecstasy,
To leave them what I have dreamt of many a day.
We must leave the happiness they deserve.

Tom Langmead (12)
St Peter's High School, Burnham-on-Crouch

Racism

Why are people racist?
Are they jealous
Or do they wish that was them?
Everyone is different in their own way
In my dream everyone gets on well
You can still play with them and be their friends
I have a dream that people do not bully other people.

Curtis (12)
St Peter's High School, Burnham-on-Crouch

World Peace

I have a dream that illnesses will be cured
And that everyone can live in a world without problems
And there will be no need for arguing
A better future for all, and a great life for everyone
Yes, I dream what everyone dreams for,
World peace.

Abigail Rolfe (13)
St Peter's High School, Burnham-on-Crouch

I Have A Dream

I have a dream,
That there is no hunger,
No drugs,
No homeless people.

I have a dream,
That everyone has equal food,
Think of the people,
African,
Indian, most starve to death.

I have a dream,
All people think the same,
No racism,
White and coloured people,
Together,
All equal.

I have a dream,
Peace over the world,
No war,
No more,
Nothing to fight for.

I have a dream.

Alice Tavinor (12)
St Peter's High School, Burnham-on-Crouch

Stop Changing

We fight about religion,
We fight about creed and colour,
Do you realise what
This world fights about?

People judge,
People bully,
Most importantly people,
Take life for granted.

People take life,
As if it was always
Going to stay,
But people don't realise.

Anything can happen
When you're sent out,
People have to face
The truth of how
Your life could end, just like that.

We fight about religion,
We fight about creed and colour,
Do you realise what,
This world fights about?

Madison Butler (12)
St Peter's High School, Burnham-on-Crouch

War

I have a dream that no more people will die.
There is no reason for people to kill or die.
People could live in a world of peace.
Children could live with their mums and dads.
Women could stay with their family.
And men wouldn't have to risk their lives.
There is no reason for war and deaths!

Megan MacLaine (13)
St Peter's High School, Burnham-on-Crouch

Imagine, Forgive, Forget

Imagine the world, poverty, hungry, homeless people,

Imagine a fresh new start,
Everyone in peace, think about the animals dying
From pollution.
Is the world really like that?
Who would want a cruel, loveless world?

No one.
But now forget the horrid, cruel world and start
Fresh, one fresh start, because everyone needs love,
Shelter and peace.
Forget the animals are dying, and help them to
Survive, to stay alive.
Forget all the countries in the world, now imagine,

One country, one world.
Filled with peace, love and no war.
Forgive all the cruel, horrid people; let them help you
Save the world.
Let everyone make the world a better place, lots of
Love and no war.
Forgive pollution and poverty,
Forgive the world.

Kira Anderson (11)
St Peter's High School, Burnham-on-Crouch

My World

M aybe one day
Y ou will learn

W e might have a quiet life
O r live with noise and chaos
R emove headaches and migraines by removing noise
L ive a quiet life, please
D ear God, please make this true.

Daniel Bill (12)
St Peter's High School, Burnham-on-Crouch

Change Your Ways!

I went to bed early one night
But then woke up in a terrible fright.
The Earth was falling towards the sun
My dream had woken me like a gun.
Am I sure it was a dream
My eyes were watering like a stream.
I quickly got out of bed
And pulled the curtains, the sky was red
I had stopped breathing, so I thought,
My mind was very distraught.

The Earth was getting hotter
We could not stop her
Unless we changed our simple ways
And recycled instead of throwing away.

Climate change was taking over
The animals were frightened, moreover
Can humans change the Earth?
They had spoilt it with mirth
And now every living thing was not a winner.
The ozone layer was getting thinner.

So listen to me or ruin the Earth for all eternity.

Victoria Peterson (12)
St Peter's High School, Burnham-on-Crouch

My Dream

M y dream is to go to college for a
Y ear or two

D esign the house I live in by
R unning a new clothing brand so I can
E arn a lot of money
A nd live somewhere hot, but
M ost of all to live a happy life, whatever I do.

Sophie Bache (14)
St Peter's High School, Burnham-on-Crouch

31

Patch's Story

Patch was a dog with half an ear,
Because of this, he couldn't hear,
His owners dumped him in a ditch,
And drove off without a glitch.

The rain came down and turned to snow
Where his owners went he did not know
He struggled a lot and yelped and yelped
When a lady bent down to help.

'What's this, who could be so vile?
I'll take you home, we'll make each other smile.'
She took Patch home and by the fire he sat
She cares for him and now that's that!

Patch is a lucky one
Who came in a million to one
There are so many mistreated dogs,
So small and helpless and left in fogs.

They do not deserve to be so mistreated,
Left alone in rain and sleet,
There's a message here, can't you see?
Stop animal cruelty!

Lara Stewart (11)
St Peter's High School, Burnham-on-Crouch

War

What is the world coming to?
People die for freedom and you,
Guns are firing all the time,
Whilst they are on the frontline.
English, Scottish, Welsh and Irish do all the best
For people around us and all the rest.
One day this war will stop
And then people won't get in a strop!

Reggie Powell (13)
St Peter's High School, Burnham-on-Crouch

One Big Country

Think of all those lonely people,
In a country of their own.
Only if there was one,
They wouldn't be alone.

There would be no homeless,
There would be no greed,
Everyone the same,
No more poverty or shame.

All one big country,
No more than one another,
There would be no wars
Don't be so mean about creed or colour.

All just one big family,
Put together as one,
They take the world for granted,
When we are all the same.

Think of all those lonely people,
In a country of their own,
Only if there was one,
They wouldn't be alone.

Katie Whitley (12)
St Peter's High School, Burnham-on-Crouch

My World

Gather all the people
Living in poverty
Give them what we got.
There's enough to share
Give them somewhere to sit
Give them something to eat,
Gather all the people
Living in poverty.

Nealie Deacon (12)
St Peter's High School, Burnham-on-Crouch

33

I Have A Dream

I have a dream,
To make an impression,
To get this world,
Out of depression.

I have a dream,
To rid the world of cruelty, greed and hunger,
To eliminate violence and crime,
To make it a safer place for older and younger.

I have a dream
That the fighting countries in the war,
Would drop their guns,
Instead of dropping dead on the floor.

I have a dream,
For everyone to be friends,
To make it real
Before my time ends.

I have a dream,
To share with you,
To share with the world
I just hope they all come true.

Georgina Lowe (12)
St Peter's High School, Burnham-on-Crouch

Just Try!

Many people have tried
But never succeeded
This is a large issue
Black and white should mould into one
A man who will always be worshipped
Having rights are all we wants
Please help resolve the issue
Just try!

Sarah Murfitt (12)
St Peter's High School, Burnham-on-Crouch

34

Do You Wish?

Do you wish, like me,
The sound of guns on the battlefield
Was silenced forever?

Do you wish, like me,
That children that have been abused
Can be happy and carefree?

Do you wish, like me,
That coloured people weren't tormented?
We are all the same inside.

Do you wish, like me,
The news wasn't filled
With sad stories of poverty?

Do you wish like me,
That mothers weren't greeted with their child upset
From cruel remarks?

Do you wish, like me,
That the world was free of this sadness
And that everyone could be at peace
Together?

Laura Broughton (12)
St Peter's High School, Burnham-on-Crouch

What's The Point Of Races?

What's the point of races?
We're all the same
If you have a problem
They're not to blame.

What's the point of races?
You can still play with him
There isn't any difference
Just slightly different skin.

Bradley Ramsey (11)
St Peter's High School, Burnham-on-Crouch

Animals On Earth

Dogs, ducks, cats, cows, rabbits and horses too
All have to be ill, just so you can look cute
Animals always suffer while humans get the goods
Read the label, check it twice
Trust me, you will feel so nice.
Non-dermatological testing is the way,
To a nice happier day
Save the animals, be a saint
Turn around and shout 'hooray'
Think of all the animals that you saved
No more animals going through pain
If you were an animal how would you feel?
If you had beauty products and gel tested on you every day
Thank you for helping me make my point
Let the pigs go around freely squealing *oink*
Don't let them be hunted
Don't let them fall
Because all animals
Big or small
They are all
                Beautiful!

Lauren Poyntz (11)
St Peter's High School, Burnham-on-Crouch

I Had A Dream

I had a dream
That the world would become a better place
For everyone
No fighting and no bullying
No weapons to kill with no money we could not afford
To get food or drinks to keep us in shape.

I just wish that there was nothing to kill
Only to survive.

Demi Searles (11)
St Peter's High School, Burnham-on-Crouch

How The World Could Be

Imagine,
Imagine how the world could be,
If everybody were carefree.
Imagine,
Imagine how the world could be,
If everybody realised the colour of skin
Makes no difference,
We are all the same.
Imagine,
Imagine how the world could be,
If there was an end to poverty.
Imagine,
Imagine how the world could be,
If children had no fear to live in anymore.
Imagine,
Imagine, how the world could be,
If all the countries were at peace,
The sounds of guns on the battlefields
Were no more.
Imagine how the world could be.

Ella Dennerley (12)
St Peter's High School, Burnham-on-Crouch

Family

I have a dream that everyone in the whole world can help each other,
And can give to those who need it the most.

I have a dream that no more than one
Dies from dirty brown water.

I have a dream that there is world peace
So no more fighting or swearing.

I have a dream that kids don't get taken away from their families.

I have a dream that more people can have the same dreams as me.

Louise Pierpoint (12)
St Peter's High School, Burnham-on-Crouch

Our World

In our world
Nothing is right
People eating too much
People eating not enough
People dying
Over something silly
That never should have happened
People homeless
With no food or drink
Other people wasting food
And not thinking anything of it
Not even sparing
The littlest thing
People with no respect
People disrespecting animals
When everything and everyone should be
Treated they way they want to be
Treated themselves
People making you feel bad
People feeling really sad.

Nadine Smith (12)
St Peter's High School, Burnham-on-Crouch

Think About Someone Else

Poor little boy sitting all alone.
No money, no family, all his friends are dead.
He pleads for some money for food.
But everyone just ignores him.

A rich, wealthy man is walking down the street.
A good life, good wife and also good kids
He sees a little boy sitting on the road
He says to himself, 'Just another one of those orphans,
No point in helping him.'

Sam Barr (12)
St Peter's High School, Burnham-on-Crouch

I Can Imagine A Better World . . .

I imagine
People shouldn't smoke,
Then no one would get ill
Nobody should attack with knives
Then no one would die,
People shouldn't take drugs
Then no one would become addicted,
The world would be a better place.
Nobody should stab
And then no one would be in jail
There wouldn't be a separation in
White people and black,
They are just the same as each other
There would be no hatred,
Just love,
The world would be a much happier place,
People over the world would get along,
And there would be no wars.
People would not have arguments or be offensive to others.
I can imagine a better world!

Megan Plumb (12)
St Peter's High School, Burnham-on-Crouch

Have You Ever?

Have you ever
Imagined something great?
Or something bad stopping?
Like crime, racism or hunger,
I have.
Imagine that we were
Rid of crime,
Like stabbing, theft and assault,

Please stop crime *now!*

Oliver Cridland (12)
St Peter's High School, Burnham-on-Crouch

I Had A Dream

I had a dream one day
That everything would go away
Guns, bullies and horrible things
Would never have been invented.

I had a dream that culture to culture
Would join up one day.
No racism or bullies
Just happiness and peace.

I had a dream that all of the polluting
Would just go away
And never come back and never come.

I had a dream
That our world would not be filled
With rubbish and clutter
Just clean fields.

I had a dream
That our world
Would become a better place.

Angel Di-Capite (11)
St Peter's High School, Burnham-on-Crouch

I Have A Dream

I have a dream that can't be seen.
I have a dream that I believe.
I have a dream to keep the world clean.
I have a dream that all children were seen.
I have a dream that child abuse had a stop.
I have a dream that hunger would end and peace would come.
I have a dream the world was full of love.
I have a dream that nastiness would end.
These are all my dreams,
And I hope yours are the same.

Shannon Bullen (12)
St Peter's High School, Burnham-on-Crouch

40

I Have A Dream, Martin Luther

He was a freedom fighter
Trying to appeal for rights,
To make their world brighter
So blacks were equal to whites.

Martin Luther King, what a guy
Always thinking of peace
The race gave a sigh
When he fought for a release.

Martin Luther had a dream
When blacks were being chained
Their skin would not be judged by creed
And their colour would be no more maimed.

This view came at a price
All the suffering had to be worth it,
He would be shot twice
But the moral of this tale is
Fight for what is right,
Don't ever quit.

David Boyd (12)
St Peter's High School, Burnham-on-Crouch

Recycle Now

R ecycling is great for the world, the
E nvironment needs help
C an't you use the bin?
Y ou know how to
C hewing gum on pavements
L ittering's what it's called, so if
E veryone would just recycle!

N early everything's recyclable, the
O zone is dying, it's everyone's
W orld so recycle now!

Kenny Harber (11)
St Peter's High School, Burnham-on-Crouch

Down With . . .

Down with war, drought,
Famine and flood.

Down with bullying, gangs
Discrimination and racism.

Down with cruelty, hunting,
Torture and abuse.

Down with drugs, crime,
Murder and robbery.

Down with genicide, homicide,
Suicide and slaughter.

Down with terrors, destruction,
Dictators and hate.

Down with tanks, bombs,
Guns and soldiers.

Up with peace, unity,
Freedom and salvation.

William Francis (13)
St Peter's High School, Burnham-on-Crouch

I Had A Dream

I had a dream that I could fly in the sky with the birds and planes.
I would fly so high that I would be able to touch the moon and stars,
And to be able to watch the butterfly flutter by
And the stinging bees.
I would be flying so high, that I could see all the pretty colours upon
                                              the ground,
The people would wave as I flew by,
Saying, 'I wish I could fly.'
And I saying, 'Just dream it and it just might happen.'
8.30 I woke up and said, 'I wish I could fly.'

Sophie-Leigh Royce (11)
St Peter's High School, Burnham-on-Crouch

A Dream

A dream is to be nurtured
A dream is to be cared for
A dream is not a dream if you don't believe in it.

Dreams are the future
Dreams are the past
Dreams are the present
Dreams are what everyone has.

People who don't work for what they believe in
Don't have dreams
People who don't keep going, don't have a dream.

A dream isn't a dream without work
A dream is a dream with work
People who don't work for their dreams are lazy,
People who fail and try again are amazing.

I have a dream,
A dream that everyone tries
And works for their dream.

James Sebborn (12)
St Peter's High School, Burnham-on-Crouch

But Not Telling Anyone

Going to school,
Always being pushed and shoved to the ground
But not telling anyone.
When it is lunchtime, you chat to your mates,
But you know someone is waiting for you,
Round every corner and behind every object.
It's home time.
They punch and kick you till you fall.
Before you go to bed you dread the next day.
The teacher asks me why I have cuts on my face,
But I still won't tell anyone.

Darrielle Hunt (11)
St Peter's High School, Burnham-on-Crouch

If We Were One?

If we were one, would we fight?
If we were one, would wars still rage?
If we were one, would anyone ever be hungry again?
If we were one, would we still have jealousy in our world?

If we were one, would we all be happy together?
If we were one, would hate and anger still exist?
If we were one, would animals be killed for fun?
If we were one, would people be murdered?
If we were one, would we all believe
In religion and Heaven?

If we were one, would we all feel safe being alone?
If we were one, would bullying and cruelty still happen?
If we were one, would we all be afraid of the dark?

I think if we were one
Nobody would have to be scared,
Wars would stop and we would all finally
Be together at peace.

Chloe Shaw (11)
St Peter's High School, Burnham-on-Crouch

No War

No war, just peace here
Imagine all the peace in the world
All friends in the world
There will be no war
Only fun, no death
No body in the streets
No bodies in the rivers
No guns for anyone
No armies
No bombs, no murders, no weapons,

   No war!

Jamie Good (11)
St Peter's High School, Burnham-on-Crouch

44

Sadly

I'm here and alive
Sadly
When I think of wars
The poverty
The bullies
Sadly

I think of the animals in danger
The trees being cut down
Sadly

I think of wildlife
The birds that sing
Being bulldozed down
Sadly

Sadly I'm here
It's not the way to think
I know I should be happy
Sadly.

Clare Thurtle (12)
St Peter's High School, Burnham-on-Crouch

War

People fight,
For what reason?
For power,
Religion,
Arguments,
Why can't we stop fighting?
And act as one
Big family?
Stop shooting before
We all drop dead.

Samuel Connelly (11)
St Peter's High School, Burnham-on-Crouch

The World Is Changing

The world is changing,
Poverty is rising,
Children dying,
Adults crying,
Diseases flying.

The world is changing,
Men of both colour aren't as one,
Friendships breaking,
Families shaking,
The world at war,
What for?

The world is changing, what can we do?
Can we change?
I hope so,
Before it is too late!

The world is changing,
But not always for the best.

Brandon Hunt (13)
St Peter's High School, Burnham-on-Crouch

Black And White

Think back, think back into your past
Think, think, it's there at last
You met that boy at the park
When it was very dark
You took the mick, out of him
Only because he had different skin
He didn't show the pain he was in
He just faced the cowards with a grin
The words he finally replied with were
Black and white, what's the difference?

Alex Garrett (12)
St Peter's High School, Burnham-on-Crouch

Global Warming

What is global warming?
Is it where the world warms up?
Or is it when the world gets angry?
The icebergs are melting
And the water is rising,
Is it going to get so full up with water
That it tips out into space?
When people waste electricity
It's affecting the world,
What's going to happen to the polar bears?
They live on ice,
Will they wash away with the sea?
We can prevent it,
But some don't make an effort
Think about the lights in the room you're in,
Do you need them on?
What is global warming?
It's where the world is being destroyed.

Cecily Cole (13)
St Peter's High School, Burnham-on-Crouch

What If?

What if people had no feelings?
What if there was no gender or race?
What if you need not have to worry what you say and do?

What if there was nowhere to go?
What if there was nowhere to be?

What if there were no friends or enemies?
What if they were just people you know?

What if there was no fighting or sadness?
What if there was just playing and happiness?

What if the world could be a better place?

Matthew Newbury (13)
St Peter's High School, Burnham-on-Crouch

47

Think Of The People!

Think of the people
Out in the world
Who are ill and in hunger
Who want love and hope
Who need someone by their side
When they're wanted most.

To have something to help them
Live the life we're in
And let them see a day of this wonderful world
And let them fulfil their dream of
Living another day.

To see them smile
With happiness
And see them want
To move on
To love and to hold
At the best of times.

Alison Aspinall (12)
St Peter's High School, Burnham-on-Crouch

The War Ends

I have a dream
That there are no wars
And that the Taliban
Will surrender.

I have a dream
That the war will end
Right here, right now.

I have a dream
That there are no guns.
No fighting and no killing.
I have a dream that the war ends.

Jack Finch (13)
St Peter's High School, Burnham-on-Crouch

48

A Better Place

Make the world a better place
Make the world a better place
By judging people by their personality
And not by how they look or by their race,.

Make the world a better place
By respecting people's religion
Make the world a better place
By being one big family.

Make the world a better place
By being kind to each other
Make the world a better place
With no crime, and no killing.

Make the world a better place
By living in peace
Make the world a better place
All you have to do is try.

Ryan Davies (12)
St Peter's High School, Burnham-on-Crouch

I Have A Dream

I magine a world without . . .

H arm
A buse
V iolence
E nding

A nger

D emolition
R acism
E vil
A ggression
M y dream is to make a stand, make the world a better place.

Megan Anderton (13)
St Peter's High School, Burnham-on-Crouch

49

I Had A Dream

I had a dream,
That I was a doctor.
I have a dream
That there is no pain.

I had a dream,
That I was a teacher.
I have a dream,
That everyone can learn.

I had a dream,
That I was a carer.
I have a dream,
That everyone is well.

I had a dream,
That I helped the needy.
I have a dream,
That my help isn't needed.

Victoria Ponder (12)
St Peter's High School, Burnham-on-Crouch

I Have A Dream

I have a dream that poverty ends
Everyone has food and no one is homeless
Africa has its fair share of money.

I have a hope that global warming stops
Car fumes have gone and there are clear, sunny skies.

I have a wish where poachers stop,
And none of the animals are endangered,
Animals are not hunted or sold.

I have a thought when crime is no more
Knife crime is over and child abuse ends
Childline is not needed and jails are empty.

Samuel Park (12)
St Peter's High School, Burnham-on-Crouch

Happy

Imagine if there was no killing
No hunger for the poor
There would be no arguments
About government and law.

People would be happy
No worries or sadness
No rich or poor
Imagine if it was a happy world.

Imagine if people can get on together
Black or white
No unkindness
That would start fights.

I want a peaceful world
I hope you do too
Not too warm not too cold
Everything will be just right for you.

Lily Paciuszko (13)
St Peter's High School, Burnham-on-Crouch

Why War?

Think of all those soldiers
Who died from the bombs
Why do we still fight
Is there anything to fight for?

They bomb the innocent people
When all they do is live
So why do we keep fighting
When all we do is die?

Just think before you shoot
Why am I doing this?

So why can't we be friends?

Harry Edwards (14)
St Peter's High School, Burnham-on-Crouch

My Dream

My dream is to sail the sea with a friend,
With a fishing net and rods we would eat fish for dinner
With microwaveable chips,
With the wind blowing through our hair on a cold, autumn day.

We would sleep aboard, have a personal sailor
To steer the ship whilst being asleep,
We would stop off at different oceans
And sell our fish, so we could buy different stuff
Like ready cooked meals and other stuff like that.

It would be an adventure, but more fun,
A bit like walking through a jungle,
But it would be even more exciting,
You could look for lions and tigers
But instead it would be fishing for fish
And that is my dream lifestyle,
I hope it comes true.

Ryanjay Culff (13)
St Peter's High School, Burnham-on-Crouch

No Difference

Peace, love, no difference
That's what the world needs
Black and white, united as one
If only we could pick them out like weeds.

Fat, skinny, who should care?
Play without a problem with each other
No matter what colour hair
Or criticising their father or mother.

Tall, small, who is perfect?
Everyone needs to improve
Can't we just get along
Without any problems or having to move?

Hannah Lote (13)
St Peter's High School, Burnham-on-Crouch

Attack

At dawn the ridge emerges massed and dune-like,
In the wild sunset of the bulging sun,
Smouldering through spouts of drifting smoke that covers,

The up to no good scarred slope, and one by one,
Tanks creep and fall forward to the wire.
The barrage roars and lifts.
Then, clumsily dropped with bombs and guns and spades
                                        and battle-gear,
Men stumble and climb to meet the fierce fire.
Lines of grey, whispering faces, masked with fear,
They leave their trenches, going over the top,
While time ticks blank and busy on their wrist,
And hope, with nervous eyes and clenched fists,
Falling in mud. Men praying to stop this nightmare!

So stop all this fighting and war,
Because this world will be no more.

Michael Joslin (12)
St Peter's High School, Burnham-on-Crouch

If I Could Change The World

If I could change the world,
The Third World would be without hunger.
Poverty would be a myth,
And people would not die younger.

If I could change the world,
There would be no fighting or wars,
And with these horrors out of the way,
Happiness would open its doors.

If I could change the world,
Then I would have peace to stay,
Of course, this will to happen for a hundred years,
It could be realised today.

Richard Cunningham (13)
St Peter's High School, Burnham-on-Crouch

A Better Place

How could the world be
A better place?
And how could it improve?
Not cutting down the Earth's green trees,
Could fix its blue-green face!

How could the world be
A better place?
And how could it improve?
If everybody shared all things
The perfect human race!

How could the world be
A better place?
And how could it improve?
Just save the planet,
Make it great
It wouldn't leave a trace!

Rachel Stedman (12)
St Peter's High School, Burnham-on-Crouch

A Better World

If the world was a better place,
Everyone would be in peace,
If the human race
Stopped being at war,
The world would be at peace.

Without our hungry, homeless friends,
The world would be a better place,
We could help these starving people
By stopping the world at war.

If the world was a better place
The world could be a better place
For everyone again.

Kirsty Simmonds (11)
St Peter's High School, Burnham-on-Crouch

54

What Would It Be Like . . . ?

What would it be like if there was world peace?
What would it be like if the wars would cease?

What would it be like if the summer would never end?
What would it be like if everybody wanted to be your friend?

What would it be like if we all agreed?
What would it be like if we all planted a seed?

What would it be like if there was only one faith?
Would the world be truly safe?

What would happen if we all spoke as one?
Our hearts must weigh at least a ton.

What would happen if we all shared?
What would happen if we all cared?

The world would be truly a better place,
To prove it just see the smile on my face.

Emily Green (12)
St Peter's High School, Burnham-on-Crouch

Happiness

A perfect place
A pure place
A happy place

Not a sad place
Not a warzone
Not a conflict

More peace
More fairness
More happiness

When will there be peace
When will war stop
When will all this happen?

Joseph Sexton (11)
St Peter's High School, Burnham-on-Crouch

Stop Killing

Stop shooting
Stop booting.

Stop hitting
Stop kicking.

Stop slicing
Stop dicing.

Stop slashing
Stop gashing.

Stop pricking
Stop sticking.

Do the crime
Do the time.

Less dying
Less crying.

Craig Thorpe (13)
St Peter's High School, Burnham-on-Crouch

I Have A Dream

I have a dream to . . .

H ave peace throughout the world
A nd for all wars to stop, and to stop
V ast numbers of people from dying from diseases
E very day

A nd in my dream there is a cure

D iscrimination like racism is a crime, and
R eally should be stopped, and
E veryone should do their bit to stop it
A nd maybe we would have peace in the world, and
M aybe different cultures could help each her instead of
   Fighting. That would be my dream.

Terry Stiffell (14)
St Peter's High School, Burnham-on-Crouch

Imagine

A world,
A world with
A world with no
A world with no war,
A world with no prejudice,
A world with no religion,
A world with no killing,
A world with no judging,
A world with no criminals,
A world with no jealous,
A world with no anger,
A world with no rage
A world with no depression,
A world with no sadness,
A world with peace,

A world with peace in mind, with voices heard.

James Williams (13)
St Peter's High School, Burnham-on-Crouch

My World Dream

I once had a dream

H appiness would always be around
A nd sadness would not be a problem as it wouldn't be there
V iolent people would not be given up on, but helped and
E veryone would be peaceful and grateful. No one would be left
to go.

A stray in the world and the poor and rich would be

D ressed and treated as equals and people, not numbers
R elying on each other for help, and
E veryone would be there for support
A nd I'm still waiting for
M y world dream (I hope it comes true soon)

Nicholas Sutton (13)
St Peter's High School, Burnham-on-Crouch

No Place Like Home

No place like home,
There's no violence or abuse,
No Hell, it's up to you to choose.
To make the world a better place,
You could stop the animals and nature being chased.

No place like home,
There's no bullying or racism,
You can make a new start,
You could stop the drugs,
That way there would be no thugs.

No place like home,
With beautiful flowers,
Good and nice powers.

With everything peaceful, there's no place like home . . .
There's no place like home . . .

Chelsea Chapman (11)
St Peter's High School, Burnham-on-Crouch

My Million Year Dream

M y dream would be to live without school.
   Yer right
Y ou, me, everybody to live life right.
   Don't think so

D angers of life will be gone.
   Never will come true
R eal food will be eaten (not silly healthy food)
   No the protests are too small
E verybody will eat chocolate
   Nearly true
A nd then girls will rule the world.
   Some day
M y dream will hopefully be solved in a million years!

Amie Brown (11)
St Peter's High School, Burnham-on-Crouch

What Makes The World A Better Place?

Imagine no more drugs
Imagine no more thugs
Imagine no more money
'Coz it ain't funny.

Imagine no more riots
'Coz no one's on a diet
No Heaven, no Hell
The world on a level ground.

Imagine no lies
And no cries
Imagine no more crimes
As the world dies.

> All this will make the
> World a better
> Place.

Sandy McEwan (12)
St Peter's High School, Burnham-on-Crouch

A New World

What if . . . there was a new world
If there was a new world with no fights,
No deaths and no destruction.
Imagine a new world with world peace,
Perhaps then the wars would cease.
Imagine a world with no possessions,
Perhaps people wouldn't have nasty obsessions.
What would happen if we were all friends,
Maybe friendships would never end.
What would happen if we all shared, cared and spoke as one?

> These wishes will not come true
> If we keep
> Staring into the blue.

Dieter Green (13)
St Peter's High School, Burnham-on-Crouch

59

I Have A Dream

Dreams are extremely special,
Keep them, treasure them,
Because you never know what might come true

I have a dreamt that people of any race, religion or age
Will learn to get along,
In peace and happiness

I have a dream that abuse and violence
Will be a memory of the past

I have a dream that when I walk down the street
Everyone will have a smile,
That lights up the sky

Dreams are extremely special,
Keep them, treasure them,
Because you never know what might come true.

Katie Banner (14)
St Peter's High School, Burnham-on-Crouch

I Have A Wish

I have a wish that I could save the world.
I have a wish that someone will know.
I have a wish that someone will find me.
I have a wish that I can go to school.
I have a wish that I am free,
And I wish it all for you.
You have a wish that I am your angel.
You have a wish that I am your queen.
You wish it all for me.
We have a wish that we will meet.
We have a wish that we will live forever.
We wish it for our day and in a dream.
That's my wish to see you, and the day I do
Will be the best day in the world.

Lili Nicholls (12)
St Peter's High School, Burnham-on-Crouch

60

Children's Death

Children marching one by one,
Lining up for death.
With guns in their hands,
They stare into the face of death.
Waiting, waiting to die,
Wanting, wanting to live.
Bombs falling from the sky,
Hitting the poor children,
Wishing to live.
Mothers and fathers reaching out,
Children screaming, crying in fear.
Every 30 seconds,
One child dies.
Parents feel ashamed.
Loving parents say goodbye to loved children.

Rachel Mason (11)
St Peter's High School, Burnham-on-Crouch

All To The People

We should respect the people who make the world a better place
Because it feels really good
And also I feel sorry for the people in Africa.

Respect them, because they play a big part in our life,
So respect them.

We don't think people go through a lot
But have you forgotten the plot?

Kids getting paid that are not the right age.
The pay is ridiculous, £2 for 12 hours,
Have you forgot your power?
It's hours and hours
Buy me a bunch of flowers.

Jake Gullen (11)
St Peter's High School, Burnham-on-Crouch

Kids With Guns

Kids with guns
Don't have fun
They don't even know what they have done!
I have a dream
No kids have guns
No more of them not having fun
You shouldn't make them do something bad,
They're not the mad ones,
You are, you're sad
It's stupid what people make kids do
They make kids kill people
Bury them too!
I have a dream
No kids have guns
Then everyone can have fun!

Nathan Stephen Keeble (12)
St Peter's High School, Burnham-on-Crouch

My Imagination

Imagine the world as a better place,
Where there is a nicer human race.

There would be no more trouble,
Everyone would be an 'in love' couple.

The litter on the floor would disappear,
And the flowers will reappear.

There will be no poverty,
Nothing would be a novelty.

What if my imagination came alive?

Everyone would survive,
And live for a better life.

Kerry Van Der Marel (13)
St Peter's High School, Burnham-on-Crouch

A Child's Dream

I have a dream
That all of mankind will live together.
I have a dream
That the countries of the world will live in peace forever.
I have a dream
That no one will ever die.
I have a dream
That there will be no greed or hunger.
I have a dream
That there's no Heaven or Hell and the world will live as one.
I have a dream
That peace will take over the world
To be a better place.
One day my dream
Will come true.

Andrew Mycroft (12)
St Peter's High School, Burnham-on-Crouch

I Had A Dream

I had a dream
That we were free
Peace on the Earth for you and me
No more hardship
No more pain
People with enough food
No more wars
Peace will reign
No more money everyone shares
Everybody lives in harmony and
Everybody cares
No more pollution
So this world we can save!

Holli Rolph (13)
St Peter's High School, Burnham-on-Crouch

Imagine

Imagine if there were no murders,
Imagine if racism didn't exist,
Imagine if there was no carbon footprint,
Imagine if people didn't hunt for fun,
Imagine if the polar ice caps stopped melting,
Imagine there were, and are, no wars,
Imagine if people didn't kill themselves,
Imagine if trees were not cut down.

Imagine instead . . .

A world where people were never hungry,
A world where we all lived together peacefully,
A world where love was stronger than hate.

Nathan Martin (13)
St Peter's High School, Burnham-on-Crouch

Some People

If people understood
That it's the inside that matters.
Not colours of skin
Or if your clothes are in tatters.

You could be poor or rich,
Black or white.
But some people don't care,
They just want to make a fight.

So if we all get along
And be happy and not sad.
Everyone can be friends
And never be mad.

Naomi Mapes (12)
St Peter's High School, Burnham-on-Crouch

Bullying

Going to school for me is always bad,
They always do things to make me sad,
They push and kick me to the ground,
When I try and hide from them, they follow me around.

When I'm in class, they call me names,
They all think it's just a fun game,
I have a dream that maybe I could sleep at night,
Without them coming into my head and giving me a fright.

I wish they would just leave me alone,
Instead of laughing at me because I sit on my own,
I have a dream that they would leave me alone
Then maybe I wouldn't have to be on my own.

Alice Turfkruyer (12)
St Peter's High School, Burnham-on-Crouch

I Have A Dream

I have a dream
That one day soon
My wonderful dream
Will come true

To help the homeless
And the starving too
I know I can do that
With the help of you

We'll all get together
And raise some money
On Red Nose Day
By doing something funny!

Lola Swallow (12)
St Peter's High School, Burnham-on-Crouch

Imagine

Imagine there was no hunger
Imagine there was no fighting
Imagine there was no racism
Imagine there was no anger
Imagine the world a better place.

Imagine there was no Heaven or Hell
Imagine there was a cure for cancer
Imagine there was no religion
Imagine there was no global warming
Imagine there was no pollution
Imagine there was a better world.

It can be if we try.

Shaun Green (13)
St Peter's High School, Burnham-on-Crouch

Imagine . . .

Imagine a world with no guns and war,
A world with no blood and gore.
No Heaven or Hell,
And nothing to sell.

Peace and quiet,
No need to diet.
No one taking drugs,
And no nasty thugs.

No more 'just white',
We should all be polite,
Black and white together
Forever.

Michael Hayes (12)
St Peter's High School, Burnham-on-Crouch

Stop!

Put away the guns
Shake hands and have fun.

Stop shooting people down
Before you make your God frown.

Stop killing fellowman
With that gun in your hand.

People die one by one
Put down that gun
Repeat, put down that gun.

Stop shooting people to the floor
Hurry up, stop the war.

Harry Dye (11)
St Peter's High School, Burnham-on-Crouch

I Have A Dream

I have a dream,

H appiness and peace all around,
A ccepting people for who they are,
V engeance to come to an end,
E scape from pain and suffering,

A nd never will there be another war,

D reaming of a safer place,
R acism to come to a stop,
E veryone to be equal, and honest with no jealousy,
A nd
M aybe the world will be a better place.

Latisha Adams (14)
St Peter's High School, Burnham-on-Crouch

I Have A Dream

I have a dream of

H ow people should act in the world
A nd what they should think
V ain people find out that
E veryone is their equal

A ble to live a happy, healthy life

D reams can become reality
R eality can become dreams
E ven bad can become good in time
A happy ending for everyone?
M y dream will be in my mind forever.

Jade Youins-Martin (13)
St Peter's High School, Burnham-on-Crouch

The World: A Better Place?

The world would be a better place,
If we had respect for others,
Friends, teachers, fathers and mothers.

The world would be a better place,
If there were better laws
No more lies, trouble and especially no more wars.

The world would be a better place,
If everyone was kind,
And sooner or later we will find . . .

The world is turning into a
  Better place!

Rebecca Tatlow (13)
St Peter's High School, Burnham-on-Crouch

I Have A Dream

I have a dream

H elping everyone
A nd helping the world
V ulnerable people to be respected
E veryone helping

A lways a home for people

D reaming for wars to stop!
R acism to stop!
E scape from suffering and pain
A ccepting people for who they are
M aybe then the world would be a better place!

Ben Mumford (14)
St Peter's High School, Burnham-on-Crouch

I Have This Dream

I have this dream of a

H appy world without
A ny nuclear weapons, any conflicts where we are all
V alued as individuals
E verywhere there would be peace

A nd no fighting. I have this

D ream of a world where people know
R ight from wrong and everyone is well
E ducated, peaceful
A nd a happy planet with all
M anner of people living side by side.

Jack Garwood (14)
St Peter's High School, Burnham-on-Crouch

I Have A Dream!

That one day the world will change,
That one day the fighting will end,
That all the terror and fear will go.

Slowly and slowly it creeps away,
While people cry and cry.

There are three things I ask:
1. Why is the world like this?
2. Why is the world about killing?
3. Why is there war?

I have a dream . . .
That the world will change!

Elle Mardle (11)
St Peter's High School, Burnham-on-Crouch

Bullies No More!

I have a dream.
A dream where people can go out, go to school and learn.
Without the fear of being bullied or beaten badly in any way.
Everyone has the right to learn and be happy!
Stop the bullies right now!

Let's get these bullies to stop
Because this abuse is nasty!

Children will carry on getting bullied
Until someone sorts this out!

Punches, kicks, hits, must stop!
Let's stop it right *now!*

Hannah Francis (12)
St Peter's High School, Burnham-on-Crouch

I Have A Dream

I like many others

H ave a dream
A great dream, where
V iolence will be a thing of the past, and
E very day will be better than the last

A nd we will stop all wars so that anyone can

D ream and not be persecuted for their beliefs
R ace will not be an issue in my dreams,
E veryone can be proud of themselves
A dream because anyone can dream, and I hope that
M y dream comes true.

Joe Tavinor (14)
St Peter's High School, Burnham-on-Crouch

I Have A Dream

I magine . . . a world of . . .

H appiness
A musement
V eneraton
E quality

A t peace

D etermination
R espect
E conomical
A spiration
M y dream is this world!

Grace Gay (13)
St Peter's High School, Burnham-on-Crouch

I Have A Dream

I have a dream . . .

H appiness around the world
A world where fighting has
V anished
E veryone is cheerful

A world that . . .

D oesn't argue
R age can't be found
E veryone is
A t peace with each other
M y dream is world peace.

Ashley Brew (14)
St Peter's High School, Burnham-on-Crouch

I Have A Dream!

I magine

H aving a world
A pparent to
V iolence
E nding

A

D ream not un-
R ealistic of an
E nd to
A trocities.
M ake it happen.

Jessica Bone (14)
St Peter's High School, Burnham-on-Crouch

Poverty

I saw an old man the other day,
He looked sad.
He was pushing a trolley and holding a bag.
His clothes were worn and old, and he looked very cold.
He stopped in my path and looked at me
And he said, 'Have you got any money for a cup of tea?'
I felt sorry for him, so I gave him a quid,
He looked at me and said, 'Thanks kid.'
I thought to myself, *how lucky I am*
I would hate to be homeless like that man.
It's a shame there are people like that.
Maybe the credit crunch did that.

Jake Cope (13)
St Peter's High School, Burnham-on-Crouch

I'd Love To

In all the world I love to build
Not with house bricks
But building small studded bricks
Day and night just building,
With bricks and bricks
All different shapes and sizes
Clicking together
Building up to a beautiful model
Alone not much but build to,
Huge models with some building
In all the world I'd love to
Be a Lego model designer.

Connor Anderson (13)
St Peter's High School, Burnham-on-Crouch

I Have A Dream

I have a dream, dream, dream
I played football, ball, ball
I kicked the ball I scored, scored, scored
I had won the cup, cup, cup
I was famous and rolling in cash, cash, cash
I went to London for a football match, match, match
But then I saw, saw, saw
The lonely, the poor people who needed money,
Needed a life
But then they vanished, gone, gone, gone –
I realised they were dead, dead, dead.
And gone.

Oliver Brown (11)
St Peter's High School, Burnham-on-Crouch

Friends

Imagine all the people who would share
We would be kinder and fair,
If we could all get along,
Everyone would be friends.

Imagine everyone being kind,
You would seem to find
All of us would be happier
If we all were friends.

Wouldn't it be great?
No more sorrow,
No more hate.

Adam Woodley (11)
St Peter's High School, Burnham-on-Crouch

I Have A Dream

Have a dream
There are no guns in the world
No knives either.

No countries are at war
They are at peace
No poachers to kill the animals
So none are harmed
No bombs to kill
No bullets to hurt people.

Ian Smith (12)
St Peter's High School, Burnham-on-Crouch

J My Poem

Recycle everything we use.
Even tins, cardboard and plastic.
Make your world much better
So we keep healthy.
Recycle rubbish, even food
Water, glass and metal.
Every time we recycle
A clean place it is going to be again.
Recycling is very healthy, helping people clean up.

James Swinger (14)
St Peter's High School, Burnham-on-Crouch

No More Bullying

I have a dream to stop bullying
Everywhere in schools and out
So anyone can go outside or inside
Not worrying about anything
Any bad thing that is happening
Or will happen, I wish would go.
Bullying isn't brave
No one likes getting bullied
So don't do it.

Jay Sadler (12)
St Peter's High School, Burnham-on-Crouch

Drugs Are Bad

Drugs are bad and have a bad taste
Drugs are sad and have no space
Drugs are making money waste
Because drugs are for mugs
But there's nothing wrong with jugs
But drugs are for thugs
So give up now
And stop, otherwise it takes out your colour
And you go pale.

Dean Wallace (13)
St Peter's High School, Burnham-on-Crouch

I Know

I know what is happening, the suffering, the war.
I know what's happening, the homeless, the poor,
I know the people that sit alone,
No place to call their home,
I know.

Luke Toms (11)
St Peter's High School, Burnham-on-Crouch

My I Have A Dream Poem

I have a dream that one day I will defy the limits in technology
And science like no one has ever done so before.
Marconi, Edison, Baird, I will make them fall to the floor.
When someone's intelligent, you nickname them 'Einstein'.
When I get to the top of my game the nicknames name will be mine.
You know, when it comes down to English I'm not exactly a whiz.
Since I've been little though, I've always wanted to be in showbiz.
When it comes to poems I'm not the bee's knees,
But can you like it? Pretty please!

Max Beard (12)
St Peter's High School, Burnham-on-Crouch

I Have A Dream

I have a dream
That the world will
Be in peace, and the
Wars will end, so that
Some people can fend,
No more people will die,
And families will be in shame
Just so other countries get some fame,
I have a dream to change the world . . .

Frankie Astell (13)
St Peter's High School, Burnham-on-Crouch

When You're Lonely

When you're feeling lonely don't be feeling sad.
Find someone deep in yourself only you can find that person.
It's your life, only you can live it
No one else exists, not even the bullies,
Just imagine a world without them.

Carrie Feagan (12)
St Peter's High School, Burnham-on-Crouch

Change

I have a dream of change,
Of the general public's power,
It won't ever rain,
But still, the plants will flower.

I know this can happen,
If we all just work together,
Things can really change,
From now until forever.

Tom Calvert (13)
St Peter's High School, Burnham-on-Crouch

My World

T rees are not cut
H ouses are built with recycled materials
E at healthily and exercise

W eather varies no global warming
O ur world without violence
R id of factories, now home made things
L ive smoke free
D reams will come true.

Hannah Lloyd (12)
St Peter's High School, Burnham-on-Crouch

John's Poem

The world would be a better place
If black and white could share the space,
No need to fight or go to war,
Cos what is all the fighting for?
The world would be better free of crime,
To not have to live in rubbish and grime.

John Turner (11)
St Peter's High School, Burnham-on-Crouch

Hol'z World

H ollie's world
O f chocolate
L ots of bears and zebras

W orld of Hollie has an
O strich that likes
R ice pudding and
L ollipops and eats up the
D ining table.

Hollie Jenkins (11)
St Peter's High School, Burnham-on-Crouch

I Have A Dream

Where nature runs free from poachers
So no animals are harmed

No testing on them
So they can live
And multiply
Like the circle of life
Where snakes can slither on the forest ground
Like water in a stream.

Christopher Hawkes (11)
St Peter's High School, Burnham-on-Crouch

Dreams

D ay by day people would get along
R acism, no people would know that is wrong
E ager to help each other through good times and bad
A nd people would appreciate what they had
M ummies and daddies, becoming every day
S o come on people, let's keep it this way!

Katherine Watts (13)
St Peter's High School, Burnham-on-Crouch

I Have A Dream

I have a dream that I will be awarded a medal
For saving someone's life in wartime.
It will be hard and will be a struggle,
But I will pull through in the end.
In my dream, I will encounter
Some horrific and wartorn places and faces,
But I will be successful and triumphant
In my hours of praise and glory.

George Gilbert (12)
St Peter's High School, Burnham-on-Crouch

To Stop Bullying

I have a dream that bullying will stop
So that people can go outside without getting bullied.
If bullying stopped that would be my dream.
I would want bullying to stop at schools and out of school.
Bullying should stop everywhere
Because people don't like to get bullied
And if bullying stops, people will not be scared
To go outside or to school.

Macauley Joy (12)
St Peter's High School, Burnham-on-Crouch

A Better World!

The world should live for love,
Live for peace, Heaven and hope,
Live for our families and friends,
And for the love that they give.
My only wish is that,
The world is free from evil,
And the things that make us cry.

Amy Tucker (13)
St Peter's High School, Burnham-on-Crouch

80

Dreaming

I'm dreaming of a better day,
No Heaven or Hell in any way,
No bullying, no violence,
Only peace, forever silence,
No killing, no dying,
Only jokes and smiling.
Maybe one day I'll get my way,
And all the fighting will go away.

Amy Gates (12)
St Peter's High School, Burnham-on-Crouch

The War

The wars are getting mad,
It should all stop,
It's getting too bad.
All the children with their guns,
All the parents missing their sons,
All the bodies lying on the floor,
All the people begging for no more,
Everyone join together and stop the war.

Martin Greene (12)
St Peter's High School, Burnham-on-Crouch

Solving A Problem?

Many people don't care,
About what's happening in the world.
People don't listen
The Earth is getting hotter
This can easily be resolved
Making the world hot is not a good thing
Animals suffering by the heat in cold places.

Anna Gilbert (12)
St Peter's High School, Burnham-on-Crouch

Bullying

When you're feeling lonely
You need a helping hand
Always look behind you
There is always someone
To keep you on the ground,
So don't ignore the bullies,
The bullies should ignore you,
There's always someone good, lying inside you.

Amy McKay 12)
St Peter's High School, Burnham-on-Crouch

Heal The World

Let the conflict wash away
And happiness and peace wave over day after day.
Let the world regenerate from execution and suffering,
Please stop this pain and let it recover from it.
Many people are crying out for no more pain and no more sorrow.
Let the people of the world come together
And stop pain and conflict and murder and war,
Stand against it and give peace and happiness.

Buster Harris (11)
St Peter's High School, Burnham-on-Crouch

Imagine . . .

I t's easy to imagine there's no Heaven
M aybe you should try
A world where religion is no more
G reed or hunger too
I magine there are
N o countries
E veryone is equal.

Rachel Pursey (13)
St Peter's High School, Burnham-on-Crouch

82

War

War should stop, as fast as light
But come to think of it, it's not a pretty sight
Although many people died in the past
They're at peace at last.
War is like a blood bath ready to overflow
People say that it's worse than that, you know
War should stop
So should the lives that are lost.

Alexandra Middleton (12)
St Peter's High School, Burnham-on-Crouch

Poem

The world would be a better place
If there were no gangs and no guns on the streets.

The world would be a better place
If there were no drugs and no smoking.

The world would be a better place
If there was no bullying
And you were only allowed a little bit of alcohol.

Ted Sims (12)
St Peter's High School, Burnham-on-Crouch

War

Horrid, horrid war
It is like a sore
On mankind
So see if you can find
Kindness in your heart
So we can start
Being nice.

Jordan Marciniak (11)
St Peter's High School, Burnham-on-Crouch

War

W hy do people let it go on?
A re people unhappy with it?
R uined lives because of it.

W hy doesn't someone make it stop?
A person's brother or sister dies.
R idiculous idea it is.

Why can't war just stop?

Charlie Mead (11)
St Peter's High School, Burnham-on-Crouch

My World

M y world is so great
Y ou would like to here

W ould you do sports
O r would you play with the animals?
R eally, really fun
L ive here for a week
D on't leave, play some more.

Scott Woloszczuk (11)
St Peter's High School, Burnham-on-Crouch

My World

M akes people happy to go
Y ou can enjoy life better

W anted signs no longer exist
O h as well, there's no smell around
R ead quietly and you won't get distracted
L oud noise won't occur
D efend your world and make it like this!

Pierce Newton (12)
St Peter's High School, Burnham-on-Crouch

84

Imagine

Imagine a place where peace is achieved.
Imagine a place where there are no criminals.
Imagine a place where there is no racism.
Imagine a place where children are safe.
Imagine a place where worries are gone.
Imagine a place where threats have vanished.

Imagine this world.

Toni Bacon (13)
St Peter's High School, Burnham-on-Crouch

Racism

Racism is a bad thing
Racism is happening all of the time
It gives people an emotional sting
Racism makes you pay a fine.

Everyone is the same
All I dream of is for all of
This racism to go away.

Joe Groom (13)
St Peter's High School, Burnham-on-Crouch

Types!

You may be Emo,
You may be a Grebo,
But we all have the same insides.

We may dress different,
We may feel different,
We are different,
No matte what type you are.

Ellie Patmore (14)
St Peter's High School, Burnham-on-Crouch

My World

M y world would have
Y ummy sweets for dinner

W ith crisps for breakfast and
O nion rings for lunch
R uling the world would be me
L iving in a house with bags of money and
D rawings of me everywhere.

Alfie Bailey (12)
St Peter's High School, Burnham-on-Crouch

My World

M y world
Y ou can help

W e can help
O verworked, underpaid people
R oaring oceans
L ightning, rain, sun and snow
D ay 'n' night.

Sophie Bowyer (11)
St Peter's High School, Burnham-on-Crouch

My Poem - Dogs And Cats

Dogs and cats all over the world
Are left outside to fend for themselves.
Biting and scratching is a way of life,
For these animals they become a fright,
Animal control comes with nets and cages,
To catch the animals for permanent re-homing.

Brooke Bell (13)
St Peter's High School, Burnham-on-Crouch

Imagine . . .

Imagine a world with no guns
No fighting or having to live in slums.
Imagine a world with no war,
With nothing else worth fighting for.
Imagine a world with no drugs,
With no annoying little bugs.

Conor Youins-Martin (11)
St Peter's High School, Burnham-on-Crouch

Knife Crime

Knife crime can ruin people's lives
It might be a part of your family
Or a good mate who has been stabbed
It could ruin you and your family
So look up and stop the knife crimes.

Sherise Ritzka (12)
St Peter's High School, Burnham-on-Crouch

Bullying

Bullying happens by people taking the mick out of you.
About your skin, hair, race, body.
Some people stay at home to get away from bullying.
And we all wish bullying would
        Stop!

Frankie Gore (12)
St Peter's High School, Burnham-on-Crouch

I Have A Dream

Since I was ten years old,
I have had a dream,
To be world champion,
And to join the best team.

I've now turned fifteen years old,
I'll take you through the whole story,
I was riding my brand new cart,
To me, my story is not at all boring.

My dad took me to a cart championship,
I was really good
I really wanted to win
Everyone thought I would.

I was at the last corner,
I was in second place,
Everyone was cheering me on,
It was a challenge to face.

I am now at the top of my career,
Carting has been fun,
Ron Dennis signed me for McLaren
I'm now driving in Formula One!

I have done well this season,
But not well enough,
At twenty four, I have to finish first,
It will certainly be tough.

The car in front went too wide,
This was my final chance,
My foot is flat out on he throttle,
I am getting ready to pounce!

My name is Lewis Hamilton,
Make sure you take a glance!

Tom Nash (12)
The Boswells School

I Have A Dream!

I have a dream
To stop famine
Thinking about them suffering
Makes me feel lonely in my own dark world
I hope my dream will come true.

I have a dream
To stop famine
We're treating them like dirt.
An animal at the bottom of a food chain
I hope my dream will come true.

I have a dream
To stop famine
Day after day they're trying to survive.
Year after year over 100,000 children die!
I hope my dream will come true.

I have a dream
To stop famine.
To let them live another day.
To let them live a future of happiness.
I hope my dream will come true.

I have a dream
To stop famine
To not let them live in starvation
But to let them live in comfort
I hope my dream will come true.

So stop spending money
On buildings and start helping
Those in Africa and Asia.

I have a dream . . . and

It will come true!

Danuelle Paynter (12)
The Boswells School

I Have A Dream

I have a dream that I will become a
Professional footballer.

I have a dream to give loads of money
To charity to try and stop illnesses
Biting at people.

I have a dream to help people less
Fortunate than me and help them
Pursue their dreams or give money so
They can survive or stay healthy.

I have a dream to have the same
Determination and self-belief as
Wayne Rooney so I can be helpful to
The world and the people inside it.

I have a dream that I can be noticed
By the public and encourage them to
Give some of their money to charity,
Inspiring smaller children to give a
Little bit of their pocket money to
People less fortunate than they are.

I have a dream that I can make a
Difference in this world and stop as
Many people dying like a painful punishment.

I have a dream that I can make all the
Children stop *crying* and turn it
Into *laughter.*

Christopher Wright (12)
The Boswells School

Freddie Mercury

He was a musical inspiration,
Who sadly passed away,
His songs live on forever,
People sing them everyday;

His style was unique,
And his dress sense very odd,
But all his fans loved him
And now he sings with God;

I wish I could have seen him,
And his band called 'Queen'.
I would have been hysterical,
And probably caused a scene;

I really like his music,
My favourite is 'Best Friend',
There's nobody quite like him,
It's a shame it had to end;

Freddie was a legend,
He loved to entertain
His voice was as smooth as chocolate mousse,
And his pitch like a runaway train;

Freddie is my hero,
Although he died of AIDS
He will live on forever,
Through the music that he made.

Georgia Rainsby (11)
The Boswells School

I Have A Dream To Cure Coughs And Colds

Cough, cough, sneeze, sniff, sniff, wheeze
Aching bones and aching head it takes all my effort to get out of bed.

Cough, cough, sneeze, sniff, sniff, wheeze
Off to school and study hard, science is just the card;
Learn about body and vitamins germs and viruses.

Cough, cough, sneeze, sniff, sniff, wheeze
Home from school in the cupboard again . . .

Cough, cough, sneeze, sniff, sniff, wheeze
Medicines I take and try so hard
Bu the amounts look sc big and long like a game of charades.

Cough, cough, sneeze, sniff, sniff, wheeze,
Medicines that doctors have made
And when you take them they sound like a parade.

Cough, cough, sneeze, sniff, sniff, wheeze,
When nightfall comes and I am looking out of the window,
Stars are glaring at me as if to say . . .

Cough, cough, sneeze, sniff, sniff, wheeze
Then when university starts and beat adversaries like
Louis Pasteur, Fleming and Marie Curie
But I will research continuously to find out how to cure a
Cough, cough, sneeze, sniff, sniff, wheeze.

Megan Scott (12)
The Boswells School

Believing In Yourself

Believing in yourself is having confidence in yourself.
When believing in yourself you can go for all of your dreams.
To believe in yourself you have to believe that you can do it.
If you believe in yourself, you need to have hope.

Sam Holloway (11)
The Boswells School

92

I Have A Dream . . .

I have a dream with,
Inspiration, devastation,
You will never know,
What way to turn, right or left?
What way should I go?

I have a dream,
When I'm floating,
In the deep, dark sea,
A great adventure for you and me.

I have a dream,
Full of death,
My pet has been put to rest,
I'm so scared. Who will be next?

I have a dream,
Full of wonder and excitement
I've just won the jackpot
I'll spend it on a new baby's cot.

I have a dream,
Full of inspiration, devastation,
You will never know,
Which way to turn, right or left?
What way should I go?

Charlotte Wright
The Boswells School

I Have A Dream

No more pain on little ones faces
Only happy days filled with fun
Full tums and happy mums
Lots of smiling faces, singing and having fun
No more lost mums and guns
The Red Nose Day gang would have won

Bradley Clarke (11)
The Boswells School

I Have A Dream

War, prison, hunger, death
Just because I am a different religion,
Just because I am a different race
But we're not so different

My pain is like a never-ending black hole
My tears are as deep as the sea
My life is as empty as space
My sadness is as unbearable as living another day

I need someone to hear my voice,
I'm not invisible
I'm not different
I'm just left out

I need hope
Something I know I can rely on
Friends who love me for who I am
Just a little shoulder to cry on

We can stop this
We can beat this
We can give hope,
We can work together.

We *can* change.

Lydia Brown (11)
The Boswells School

I Have A Dream

I have a dream
A cure for cancer
An illness so wicked and mean
It tears through the body
It devastates lives
Cancer is the worst to be seen.

It's killed some of my family
Cancer is cruel, callous, causing catastrophe,
It has brought great sadness to me.

Cancer is a darkness, an evil killer
It grows so fast
A cure for cancer is all I ask.

'Cheer' went the world
To one of the biggest achievements
I would be the best
And no more tearful bereavements
No more loved ones laid to rest.

I have a dream
And one day soon
Not only a dream
But this dream will come true.

Lauren Harris (11)
The Boswells School

I Have A Dream

I have a dream.
Bang bang went the bombs.
That there will be world peace.
Bang bang went the bombs.
War is black paint splashed on a blank canvas.

I have a dream.
Drip drop went the tears,
That cancer will be cured.
Drip drop went the tears.
Cancer is like a cruel weed, spreading and growing.

I have a dream.
Growl growl went his tummy.
That people won't be hungry.
Growl growl went his tummy.
Hunger is a never-ending ache.

I have a dream.
'Hooray, hooray,' went the people, the war has ended.
'Hooray, hooray,' went the people, cancer is cured.
'Hooray, hooray,' went the people, the starving have food.

And that is my dream.

Nicole Hadley (12)
The Boswells School

I Have A Dream

I have a dream that one day karate will go into the Olympics.

I have a dream that for just one day
We don't have to pay
For all the young people to show off their talent.

Then we win gold
And all goes on hold
For London 2012

I have a dream that all martial arts
Come together to one part
And they all go into the Olympics.

We all come home
Pretending the medals are as fake as foam
Then our school mates all get jealous

Then they start on us
We don't make a fuss
We just defend with our karate

We all do mawashi gens
They think we are fairies
Until they land on the floor.

Dan Tipp (11)
The Boswells School

97

Disease

I have a dream that all disease in the world is wiped out,
Disease is like a black cloth of darkness covering us all in the cold
Winter weather,
Disease is swarms of mosquitoes sucking blood like
A vampire and replacing it with disease,
Disease is like a ninja on a mission
Disease, death and dark times ahead, that is what
Happens if you get some diseases.
Mosquitoes are super suckers, sucking blood, that give you disease,
Groan, moan and sigh
These are noises you make when you are ill
Then you will ask why
It had to happen to me
How couldn't I see
But it has to be
Has to be me
But if all was gone
We would all happily live
No one would die a horrible death
And there would be lots of people left
To live life happily.

Nicola Morl (12)
The Boswells School

I Have A Dream

M other Teresa was a Roman Catholic nun with an Indian Citizenship
O ver 45 years she ministered to the sick, lonely, orphaned
   poor and dying.
T hroughout India and other countries she did charity work
   (missionaries)
H omes and hospices for people with leprosy, AIDS, tuberculosis
   She provided
E ighteen of age she left her parents home to join the Sisters
   Of Loreto
R epublic of Macedonia Mother Teresa was born

T he day she was baptised is known as her true birthday
E xtending her work was made possible for her
R eceived permission from the Holy See to start her own order,
   'The Missionaries of Charity'
E ffective help to the poorest of the poor in a number of countries
   In Asia, Africa and Latin America
S he felt strongly that God was calling her
A gnes Gonxha Bojaxhiu in Skopje, Macedonia, on August 26,
   1910 she was born.

Steffy George (11)
The Boswells School

Music Within Me

Imagine a world without music,
How dull and boring it would be,
The world would be nothing without the amazing beat,
But you could sing in your dreams,
No one has to tell you how to sing
As it's your song, not theirs,
It could be anything you like,
Like a herd of wild elephants,
Or as calm as the fish in the sea,
I couldn't imagine a world without music.

Olivia Simmons (12)
The Boswells School

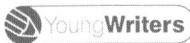

I Have A Dream

I have a dream that poverty would end and everyone would be free
That they could shower and not drink from the dirty sea
They would get and live longer than five
And have a soft, warm bed and comfort to thrive
To have clean, dry clothes and not blankets and rags
To have a certain someone to look after your health
No matter what religion or wealth
I have a dream that there is no racism
No certain skin colour you're meant to have
That you can believe in any religion
Without any criticism
That people don't laugh at you whether you are fat or thin
And not treat people like rubbish in a bin
I have a dream that the world became as one and there were
                                                    no wars
And that that one person didn't come through the doors
I have a dream and I hope it comes true.

Shailan Gohil (12)
The Boswells School

Imagine

I magine

H appiness
A ppreciation and
V ariation without judgement
E verywhere

A dream

D ifferent
R eligions in harmony
E veryone is at peace
A t last, a
M iracle.

Alex Heard (12)
The Boswells School

100

I Have A Dream To Be Like Lewis Hamilton

L ucky Lewis, loads of lolly
E asy going, happy and carefree
W ell trained, winning streak and what a racer
 I s as hard as a concrete race track and as fast as a speeding bullet
S ocial, strong and supremely cool

H istory maker
A wesome, athletic and always ready to make a move
M oney earner
 I n a league of his own, world champion
L eader of the race track
T ries hard in every race and in everything he does
O ne to beat
N o one believes more in himself than he does.

That's my dream, to believe in myself that's what I would like to do.

Ross Toomey (11)
The Boswells School

Inspiration

Music inspires me,
The way it runs through my body
Like a stomping herd of deer.
Dancing inspires me,
The way my whole body comes alive
As the music enters my ears.
Painting inspires me,
The way a beautiful mix of colours
Can make you think as you look.
Writing inspires me,
The way a weird, wonderful world
Can open up on the page of a book.
Life inspires me.

Lucy Barker (12)
The Boswells School

I Dream

Imagine a world with no music or inspiration.
Imagine, imagine what life would be like.
No fun, enjoyment or joy.
No sound, movement or life.
Imagine, imagine what life would be like.
I dream of a perfect world where there are
No wars, racial discrimination or poverty.
Imagine, imagine what life would be like.
Imagine a world that could be filled with colours and amazing
Experiences that never leave us.
Imagine, imagine what life could be like.
Imagine what life could be with happiness and joy.
Imagine, imagine what life could be.
Is this a dream?
With our help we can make it reality.
I dream.

Eden Graham (11)
The Boswells School

I Have A Dream To End All Wars

War is a life changer,
A fire which doesn't go out,
It goes on and on.

To stop the fighting,
To stop the pain and bloodshed,
It goes on and on.

Why keep killing, why?
Brings tears to broken families,
It goes on and on.

It needs peace to end,
Stop fighting and be friends,
It surely must end.

George Clements (11)
The Boswells School

I Have A Dream . . .

War
I don't like war,
I hate to see people die,
When I see their hopeless faces
It makes me want to cry.

World Peace
I like the thought of world peace,
World wars to end,
The world would be a happier place
With loads of lives to mend.

Hunger
I hate to see people starve,
The Africans, Indians and more,
They look very unhealthy,
Foods should be free from stores.

Toby Heseltine (11)
The Boswells School

Racism Is . . .

Racism is twenty stabs in the back,
Racism is salty tears running down a child's face,
Racism is misery,
Racism is a cold rainy day,
Racism is a dark soul,
Racism is a scary nightmare,
Racism is a lonely dark cave,
Racism is a broken heart,
Racism is the prick of a cold, sharp needle,
Racism is poison,
Racism is a vicious monster,
Racism is . . . *bullying!*

Abigail O'Malley (11)
The Boswells School

I Have A Dream

I have a dream that everyone
Will stop war and fighting and
Work together and help people
Who need   the help
And attention   care for
Other people   more than
Yourself. Believe in everyone
And believe in yourself. Don't be
Greedy but share what you have
Got. The person
I am describing
Is Mother
Theresa and
It was good.
World peace.

Thelma Sengere (11)
The Boswells School

The Homeless

T orture
H ealth
E nergy

H omeless people are the same as us
O nly they have less money
M eals are the things they need but can't afford
E nergy is the thing they don't have
L oss, homeless people often lose family
E very day is the same
S till waiting for someone to come
S itting alone hoping for help.

Lucy Matthams (12)
The Boswells School

I Have A Dream

I dream of being an entrepreneur, getting their money.
I dream of being a bee getting their honey.
I dream of being a fireman saving people everyday.
I dream of being a flower, blooming then going away.
I dream of being an actor reading the words and remembering
Them all.
I dream of being a Guinness World Record Holder for something
Weird, or for being too tall.
I dream of being a hero, fighting and winning a war.
I dream of being a saviour knocking on your door.

I have a dream.

James Bush (12)
The Boswells School

I Have A Dream

I have a dream that one day world peace will come together.
Together forever will keep driving us on.
That troops getting killed in Afghanistan, Iraq, we will save their lives
By pulling them out.
Al-Qaeda will realise they give no peace and no happiness
Just sadness and deaths.
If you think of all the families and lives they've destroyed
You would realise how serious this is
World peace, that's a true dream.

Peace, let it take over.

Liam Bush (11)
The Boswells School

I Have A Dream . . .

I have a dream and that dream is to stop all . . .

F alling tears streaming down their faces
A ll of the ground, dry and hard
M any people suffering
 I n desperate need of water
N othing ever grows
E mpty rumbling bellies

My dream is to stop all famine and people dying needlessly
of hunger.

Georgia Williams (11)
The Boswells School

I Have A Dream

I have a dream that one day all nations will drop their weapons
And stop their destruction.
I have a dream that one day all wars will end
And people will love and hug.
I have a dream that one day all nations will unite as one.
I have a dream that one day death is caused not by man
But by natural causes.
I have a dream that one day people should not think about
self but we.
I have a dream that one day people can live good, healthy lives.
I have a dream that one day no one is poor or hungry.
I have a dream that one day the rich will give to the
needy and charities.
I have a dream that one day trees will be cut down only for what
we need.
I have a dream that one day man will not be cruel to animals.
I have a dream that one day pollution will become history.
I have these dreams because one day I hope the world can be
at peace.

Cedric Percy Sam (13)
The Campion School

My Dream

I want to work
As a rock star
Or maybe I'll go
And travel afar.

I want to base jump off a cliff
Surf the biggest wave
Be the best at race driving
Or discover the biggest cave.

I want to find
An amazing cure
For all the disease
So life can be pure.

I want to enforce
The fairest of laws
And to be the person
Who can give to the poor.

I want to run many miles
Row for the GB trials
Play rugby for the England team
And row like a machine.

I'll never turn to drugs
Or easily be mugged
I want to be clean
So I never go mean.

I want to be a mathematician
Or be a musical magician
I want to be able to write
That'll keep you up all night.

I now wake up from my darkness
But remember my dream

Miguel Naveda (12)
The Campion School

107

When Will It End?

Waiting for it to happen,
Today? Tomorrow?
Lying in bed
The colour of my cheeks faded
With my hands holding my head.

I walked down the stairs
And looked in the mirror
And noticed once again I had less hair
And my body much thinner.
When will be the end?
Today? Tomorrow?

I turn on the telly
With everyone talking about me.
My body aches all the time
I hear my name
And I feel shivers down my spine.

I think about the things I've done
The success I made
All the things I said
Soon it won't make a difference
Because I will be dead
But when? Today? Tomorrow?

When will it be over
I've done my best, I tried my hardest
All for nothing,
The end is coming
When? Today? Tomorrow?

My day is filled with silence
I am lonely in my home
I am no longer seeing violence
And one day, some day,
Today? Tomorrow?
My family will be alone.

One thing I learnt,
Live life to the full
Have no regrets

Don't be a fool, it can all go away
With one dangerous life threat.
Everyone shouted my name
My picture taken every second
I begged for some shade
My name they cried
And I said, 'Yes, it is me, Jade.'

Joseph Nelson (14)
The Campion School

I Have A Dream

My dream is different to anybody else's,
My dream I couldn't explain how much I want it,
My dream is this,
To be on the stage, no one telling me what to do.
To wake up in the morning and look forward to be doing something
I love.
I want people to look up to me and think I want to be just like him.
I'm not just in it for the money,
It's something I love doing and want to be doing,
And nobody can tell me otherwise.
I also want a happy life, no crime, no violence,
And certainly no knives.
To live in a world where no one is judged by their colour,
But by the way they are, and live and speak.
I can't help but dream,
For someday it will be a happier world
And I want to be someone who could make a change.
My dream is my goal in life,
Something I can look up to be
And just hope that if that chance would come,
I would grab onto it and never ever let go.
I'm only young and have my whole life ahead of me
And all I can ever hope and dream is that I can make the most of it.

Taylor Triphook (12)
The Campion School

I Have A Dream

I have a dream
Impossible it seems
I wasn't to be a game ranger
And a lion tamer.

I want to see the big five
And amazingly it will be live
Leopards, lions and the rest
This job is simply the best.

Taking people on a safari
Then coming home to a dinner of calamari
Meeting wonderful folks
And all the amazing jokes

I will have to study lots of books
And I think I've got the looks
Coupled with my personality
I'm going to make this a reality

Up early to see the rising sun
That's the only way to have fun
Watch the animals as they wake
That is all it is going to take

Back to the camp for a wash
Then food oh so posh
Bacon, egg and some toast
In the evening we have a roast

At dusk out on the Land Rover
I could do this over and over
It gets very cold at night
But I think it's a delight.

This is not as hard as it seems
As it is my ultimate dream.

Sam Keanly (12)
The Campion School

I Have A Dream

I have a dream,
To be a footballer,
I would always remember,
To be a goal scorer.

He has a dream,
To be a vet,
Saving animals he's met,
Saving people's pets.

She has a dream,
To be a gymnastic,
Jump then cartwheel and flick,
She would be fantastic.

They have a dream,
T o be in a music band,
Smashing the drums with your hand,
As it vibrates through the land.

A poor person has a dream,
To have some money,
To buy a house, food for their tummy,
Buy something that's funny.

A sick person has a dream,
To get well,
To get out of their hell,
Wish their life never fell.

Everyone has a dream,
Some of them don't come true,
But other people achieve,
All you have to do is believe.

John Burnham (12)
The Campion School

I Have A Dream

I have a dream,
My dream is my ambition,
What I want to accomplish in life,
I want to be a role model,
Be a great dad,
Provide for my family,
Have a wife who loves and cares about me,
I shall be rich enough to give to CAFOD,
And still treat my family,
This is the way I want to live my life,
What about yours?
It's in your own hands.
The more you learn the more you can earn,
You do not need to be clever,
To earn a lot of money,
You need to work hard,
And study,
I'm sure you can smell,
taste and hear your dream coming towards you,
I hope you grab it,
When the chance comes by,
And hold it tight,
Not to let go,
I want to complete my dream,
I shall give one hundred percent,
Until I get there,
I hope your dream comes true,
I hope you wish the same for me too,
That is the end of my poem,
But not my dream.

Liam Snellin (13)
The Campion School

I Have A Dream

I have a dream to be the cream
Not only the best but to beat all the rest
Cooking for royalty, celebrities and friends
That's right, I'm to be a chef and full of zest
Auguste Escoffier would bow in my wake
Famous as he is, his steaks no one would miss
Mine would be succulent, saucy and moist
Customers will eat mine because they have the choice
Jamie Oliver can talk and could cook any old dish
But people will come far to sample my fish
My cooking will be the talk of any fair city
Streets ahead of my friend Gary Rhodes
Delia, Gordon, Ainsley and Worrall will be taking ideas
From the new chef in town
Heston of course will be talking them down
My dream to cook in the best places in town
My signature dishes the dearest around
What I can't do with a whisk and an oven
A set of sharp knives and a Billingsgate plaice
Oh my dreams are aflow with the perfect dish
My chef whites are crisp with a sharp ironed look
Different to others as you would expect 'cause I do it to the book
I'm the nearest thing to perfection as I create new confection
Whipped cream and fruits not even an exotic dancer has seen
With mass coloured sauces, streaming with glee
And what I would do with some cheese remains to be seen
The place I've looked for no one has been
And most important of all my kitchens do sheen
What a dream!

Rory Freeman (13)
The Campion School

113

Against The Odds

Outside we are fiercely outnumbered
But is that going to stop us?
The battle maybe rough as the ground you are on
But will this blemish our spirit?

Yes, we are against the odds
But we will go out there at our best
And the best we damn should be
For when a bear captures a fish
The fish does not give up, it fights back till its last breath.

We are going out there as boys
And we shall return as men
We will return home as heroes
Defending the great walls of our country.

For we are that little bit of hope
In those children back at home
We are that tiny bit of energy
That produces a kick-out punch
For we are heroes.

The battlefield maybe infested with red flags
But we shall kill off the infection
It shall not spread any further
Than our swords and shields.

We will fight till our last breath
For we are men
For we are soldiers
For we are heroes.

George Lutterodt (13)
The Campion School

I Have A Dream

I have a dream
A place to go
One exotic land
Far away from home
Where the sun is bright
Until the night
Peace and quiet at last
Time goes by so very fast
A twinkle in my eye
Paradise above
Where I lie
Tropical fruits, tall mango trees
Raving monkeys and buzzing bees
The beat of the drum runs through my skin
I feel happy with nothing to sin
Freedom arrived
In the sea I dived
Aquatic wonders await
Dazzling fish dashing past
Great white shark
Got to go fast
This is the life
Nothing better
Who could come to write a letter
Down at the bottom of the sea
A giant octopus scaring me
Big blue whales eating freely
I swim with them joyfully.

Charlie Gillespie (12)
The Campion School

I Had A Dream

It's getting late
It's time for bed
I lay down my weary head
Laying still I fall asleep
Into my dream I creep

In the dressing room I'm feeling proud
Outside the fans are shouting loud
Onto the pitch with the French we go
About to start this football show

The whistle goes the match has just begun
This will be a lot of fun
The French are favourites to win
But I'm running with the ball and I cross it in

Through their defence a head pops up
Puts the ball in, we are 1 nil up
The cheers of the excited crowd
Around the stadium makes me so proud

Half-time has come
We're nearly done
Back out we go
To continue the show
Let's hope we keep our lead

I open my eyes the morning is here
Did we win, it's not that clear!

James Doyle (12)
The Campion School

Inspiration

There's always someone worse off than you,
It's hard to believe when you feel so blue,
You're more concerned by the things you can't do.
There's always someone worse off than you.

So you have a disability or an illness with no cure,
It's going to stop you from achieving, of that you are sure.
Things you used to do, you won't be able to anymore.
Your self-confidence and self-image have now hit the floor!

But it's OK, you will survive,
You should be glad. You are alive!
To achieve our dream you must strive,
Belief, determination, where's your drive?

Some children in the world don't even get fed.
The terminally ill, lie waiting in bed!
'It could be worse,' it is often said.
Ask the widow, the orphan. Their loved one is dead.

So count your blessings your time isn't due.
Go out there, go on, start something new.
'Life is for living!' that statement is true!
There's always someone worse off than you!

Matthew Birtles (14)
The Campion School

The Teacher's Gift

Beneath this stone Miss Chit-Chat lies
Her gossiping days are done.
Her last words were as she passed away
I'm just dying to tell someone.

Every time I tell the time,
Or work out ten times ten.
I open a precious gift
Bequeathed to me by you.

You gave me names and numbers,
You taught me how to spell
You filled my head with goats and trolls
And tinderboxes too.

You planted seeds inside me
But did not see them grow
A bell rings at the end of school
We pack our bags and go.

These words I scrawl on paper
This shape upon my tongue.
Is made from things you taught me
Way back when I was young.

Alan Sabu Mathew (13)
The Campion School

I Have A Dream – Words To Change The World!

Imagine if you could walk alone at night,
Never afraid no longer full of fright,
No one dead no wounds to the head,
It is safe for all tonight.

Imagine if the prisons were clean,
No longer full of teens,
Who misunderstood and try as we could,
To stop all we had seen.

Imagine a mum all worried,
Sitting at home alone,
The bell starts to ring,
She drops everything,
And rushes towards the door,
She screamed and falls to the floor,
As the police walk through the door,
Imagine if this was no more.

Oliver Lee (13)
The Campion School

My Dream

I've imagined an entire world without conflict and war,
Without walking down the lonesome street
Getting beaten to the floor.

I've imagined the streets of the world to be full of peace and love,
That people respect and follow in the footsteps of the God above.

The world is like an ongoing war with no peace and care,
The world should be a peaceful place where people are treated fair.

A world of war should never be seen,
A world of love is my one main *dream*.

Jack Lilley (14)
The Campion School

I Have A Dream

I have a dream
Which will make many memories
Many experiences
Make me better
Which will show me the ways of humanity.

I had a dream and now I have
Memories of loneliness
To experience begging
Fending for myself
I've seen a rich man pass and a poor man give.

This dream gave me
Memories of togetherness
Experience of life and death
Contentment
The simple knowledge of what you give, you get.

PS Unless you're a vagrant
PPS I'm a vagrant.

Fionnan Byrne-Perkins (12)
The Campion School

I Have A Dream

I have a dream,
That every person is loved,
That no one goes hungry,
That everyone is equal,
That you and I are friends,
That you are not that boy in the corner,
That you can trust me,
That I can help everyone,
That you have the same dream.

Taylor Magner (13)
The Campion School

I Have A Dream

I have a dream,
And in my dream I was on a roller coaster,
A complete thrill ride,
Where you do loop-de-loops and one massive drop.

In that dream I realised that life should be like a roller coaster
Pumped with adrenaline,
The wind blowing through my hair,
And the thrill about knowing that it could stop at any moment.

Considering it could stop at any moment,
You should be prepared by fulfilling your life's ambitions,
Because when that ride stops and people get off, you will die,
Until someone decides to ride you.

Tommy O'Donnell (13)
The Campion School

Not To Follow Mistakes

Are you a person who likes to make mistakes
Swimming in lakes and taking unnecessary breaks?
Did you bake that awful cake
Or did you make the perfect one?

Do you like to mess about
Or do you want to sort it out?
Did you create that deadly fire
Or are you a big, bad liar?

Do you want to help someone out
Or would you rather keep it in doubt?
So stop right now and make a change,
For the better, or not, you decide.

Joshua Myner (13)
The Campion School

Bullying

The bell rang
The bullying began
The big punch
The frightful bunch.

They pulled my hair,
And the arms of my teddy bear.
They bullied me because I was small,
I really didn't like it at all.

They followed me home,
And that's when I should have known
My life was a mess,
They messed up my frilly dress.

They called me horrible names,
I was left with all the blame
They have ruined my whole life,
They threatened me with their knife.

I didn't want them to hurt me.
All I wanted was to be free.
They made me cry,
As they laughed and walked by.

The next day came,
They called my name,
'Last day of beating you today, oh don't cry!'
They hit me, beat me, and left me to die.

I lost my short life,
To their sharp knife.
I miss my mum so much,
All I want is one more touch.

The bullies took my life,
To their dreadful knife.
Don't let bullies take you too,
Stop and save the children just a few.

Bullying isn't nice,
Stop it, so it doesn't happen twice.
They ruin your life, and hurt you,

I know how it feels too.

My mum and dad cried,
They wanted me alive, they tried.
Stop it happening forever,
Stop bullying all together!

Chantelle Hurrell (13)
The King Edmund School

Normal?

In the mirror,
I can see,
Someone I never used to be,
I see a shy girl,
With nothing to lose,
A beautiful girl,
Who's down in the blues,
A girl that could reach the top of the sky,
But instead hit rock bottom when it's time to fly.
A girl who's mum stares into space,
Who gets so angry,
She gets a punch in the face,
A girl who gets beaten,
And feels so blank,
A girl who's troubled heart sank.

No one understands how this girl feels,
She loves her mum,
But the heart really kills.

The scars appear on her doll-like face,
She seems to be living life at the wrong place.

At school,
She'll be set to do a task,
But her pain is disguised by a fatal mask.
Don't hurt her anymore.

Chelsea Bush (13)
The King Edmund School

John George Gaylor

There was a man from Bethnal Green
Who's house was always clean.
He lived with his wife,
Who was young in her life,
He had two sons and one daughter.

It was the day when the news came through,
And the man was in the post office queue.
Franz Ferdinand was shot,
Gavilo Princip was not,
And so World War One had begun.

It was the day after the news came through,
And he was trying to decide what to do,
As he was brave,
He went with a wave,
And set sail in HMS Minotaur.

He worked down on the bottom deck,
And he worked without modern tech.
He stoked all day,
He stoked all the way,
And stoked until his ship was torpedoed.

He returned home later that year,
But never did once shed a tear.
He survived the war,
But found it a bore,
And died later due to his injuries.

That man's name was John George Gaylor,
He served Great Britain as a sailor.
Though his life was short,
For our freedom he fought,
That man is my great, great grandfather.

George Watkins (11)
The King Edmund School

Rats Are People Too!

Rats have feelings,
They have favourites in food,
They have their own personalities,
And have different moods.

Rats don't have diseases,
Illnesses or bugs,
They are clean, kind animals,
They are perfectly fine to hug.

In my living room,
I have three rats,
They are all different
Casper, Tokyo and Max.

Casper is the shy one,
He is grey in colour,
Casper is the runt of the litter,
When you get close he does a runner.

Max is in charge,
He has a wonky tail,
He is also grey in colour,
He will get the best bed without fail.

Tokyo is the fat one,
He is Siamese and half blind,
He is white in colour,
When he hides he is hard to find.

Rats should be treated as equals,
Not discriminated by their past,
I love rats and so should you,
Rats are here to last!

Emily Bull (12)
The King Edmund School

Understand

As I walk among the children
I see their faces,
Filled with terror.
I wonder why they look and stare,
Across the playground?

I step over there,
Walk through the crowd,
Then see this thing
All huddled up,
Shaking on the floor,
Then turn my head to see,
A person standing tall and proud,
But eyes bursting with fear.

I try to help the shaking figure,
And take them from the crowd,
So then my attention is on the bully,
What's really on their mind?

They're scared,
Scared of themselves,
And all they really need
Is for their victim to just stand up,
And help them understand,
Understand how to be free.

Holly Hutcheon (13)
The King Edmund School

Smoking

You don't look hard, you don't look big
Why would you want to put your life at risk

You could cause others misery,
Even if you don't want to.

Dylan Bond (13)
The King Edmund School

Bullying

The bell rings
It's the end of school
I feel so happy
It's the weekend at last
I walk through the gates
Then I suddenly stop, I see my fate
I see them waiting
Waiting for me.

I walk towards them
Cowering with fear
There in the distance it's their laughing I hear
I see their big grins, it's a horrible sight
Then my tummy goes tight
I know it is time for the fight.
The fight will begin.

The leader comes forward
With his gang one by one
The leader says a threat
The sun has set
With a flash
There is a bash
They run for it
I fell on the floor.

Shina McNaught (14)
The King Edmund School

127

Problems And Consequences

Oh my nan she does like to smoke
But I find it a bit of a joke
She coughs and she wheezes
She splutters and sneezes
And is starting to sound like a bloke.

Oh my dad he does like to eat
He's on a diet but I see him cheat
I think to replace it
With what people see fit
Like gum to chew to compete.

Oh my mum she does like to drink
But she can't really hear herself think
Driving is too hard
Her car was crashed after one yard
So she bought a new one which is pink.

Please don't end up like this
Your life would be more bliss
Try to stop it
Or you won't be fit
And you will never get a kiss.

Daniel Ward (11)
The King Edmund School

The Quiet One

The quiet one, alone in the dark.
Not a word is said
Scars and bruises hidden
Underneath their clothes,
Speak up, speak up.

The quiet one, who hides their fear,
Should be with others,
Understanding and caring mothers,
Who know when something is wrong.
Speak up, speak up.

The quiet one, not really alone,
Not if they speak up.
Should never have to hide
Because no one is the best or worst
Speak up, speak up.

Don't let bullies take over
Speak up, quiet one, speak up.

Jade Mott (12)
The King Edmund School

My Dream Is Being In The Team

A man from London, Chelsea
Number 26 defender John Terry,
He plays centre back
And never has a lack
Of keeping the balls out the net
Even in Asia's Tibet.
His rival defender for Man U,
Defender Gary Neville, number 2
He is the best above all the rest,
My dream is being in the team
Alongside them, I'll be seen.

Timothy South (12)
The King Edmund School

I Hear A Scream

You have a future,
That is very grand.
Far away in distant places,
The bird of peace will land.

Gunfire will cease,
Peace will ring her bell.
None shall be rude again,
Or say 'What the hell?'

Terrorists'; bombs,
Will explode in their faces.
And there will be no insults
About the nations races.

And the Lord up above,
Will be pleased with our work.
He will coax us out,
Of the shadows in which we lurk.

Michael Miller (11)
The King Edmund School

War Issues

In our world today,
We do not think how lucky we are as a country.
Just think, when we turn on our tap to have a glass of water,
All the third world countries are dying from drinking dirty water,
Which carry bad diseases.
Sometimes we take these issues for granted.

As you know, there is something always going on in the world.
Such as war.
War is one of the main issues to do with the unfortunate countries.
Mostly everything to do with war is fought because of religion.
Religion is different all over the world,
One day we all hope that war will stop.

Ben Brower (14)
The King Edmund School

Smoking Kills

Cough, cough,
You're killing yourself
Smelly, stinky
Is your breath.

Your lungs are black
Full of tar
Just like the road
That keeps your car.

The rats' poison
In your blood
Soon you will start to cry
And then there'll be a thud.

In the ambulance
Clenching your chest
When it's your funeral
You'll be wearing your Sunday best.

Jack Norman (14)
The King Edmund School

The Chains That Bind Us

Freedom is it really real or is it fake?
Oppression, a cancer that plagues the 'Free world'
Is that really real, or is it fake?
America, the international policeman prides itself with binding
Those who oppose
Freedom isn't real, it's just a lie
Oppression is everywhere
Forcing us down
Hypocrisy
Brutality
Morality
The New World Order!

Sam Kershaw (13)
The King Edmund School

My Nanny Anne Smokes A Lot

My nanny Anne smokes a lot
It really does disgust me.
Soon she will lose the plot
That won't be nice to see.

My grandad tries to tell her off
But she doesn't take notice
And all the smoke, it makes us cough
And she stinks when we give her a kiss!

My nanny is a dirty smoker
It sounds so bad to say
She thinks she's a funny joker
That smokes 40 a day!

Nanny, I wish I could help you
Inside, I am crying
I really don't know what to do,
Because slowly you are dying.

Mia Cotton (12)
The King Edmund School

The War

The war is a terrible thing
It stops people living
And lets people die
That can't be a good thing.

The war is a terrible thing
It's not fun at all
Young people get killed
From bombs falling down.

The war is a terrible thing
It makes countries hate each other
Whole races go against each other
People don't understand what to fight for.

The war is a terrible thing
It uses all our money
It uses all our people
They try and keep safe.

Billy Purkiss (14)
The King Edmund School

My Parents

M ight seem silly to you adults,
Y ou may think this song makes no sense.

P ut it to heart and think on it,
A m I really speaking nonsense?
R eady to work on my every call,
E ven when it sounds obscene.
N ot to mention making my meals,
T rying as hard as they mean.
S ounds very random but I know it's true,

R ocking the poem for me but not you.
U nder loads of pressure,
L oving as ever.
E ven to the stormiest weather,

I love my parents and they love me too,
My parents rule and I know that's true.

Serina Shelton (11)
The King Edmund School

Never Give Up

Never give up,
Even when you're stuck,
And it feels like nothing will work.

Never give up,
The future brings luck,
And sadness won't even lurk.

Never give up,
When you've run out of luck,
Good things will come.

Never give up,
Don't get stuck in the muck,
Because you're not dumb.

Lee Aylott (11)
The King Edmund School

134

Just Yelp!

There was a young guy Len
Who chose crack over his girlfriend
He loved it more
Said she was a bore
So he took it until the end.

Len was a very stressed guy
He thought it was easier to die
He hated his life
Had no kids, no wife
And his chance of life had gone, goodbye.

But Len could have got help
If only he would've got up and yelped
There are people out there
So if you're in despair
Don't choose drugs, just *yelp!*

Jasmine Zekai (11)
The King Edmund School

Never Give Up

Never give up,
Even when you're out of luck,
If you keep on trying,
And stop crying,
You will succeed!

Never stop,
When our hopes have dropped.
If people hadn't tried,
You would have died,
You will succeed!

Never give up,
Never stop,
You *will* succeed!

Alice Repper (12)
The King Edmund School

Red Nose Day

C hildren dying every day
O f malaria when a
M osquito net only costs £5
I want to change this, if you, my
C ountry will believe

R ound the world
E very day
L ots of money
I n our pockets can't we
E ven spare a penny
F or children round the world?

R ed
N ose
D ay

George Claydon (11)
The King Edmund School

President Obama

He, who had a dream helped to make this man's dream come true,
Martin Luther King is the man that did a powerful speech,
For if he didn't do this speech, the world would not be what it is now,
The man he helped is now president, President Obama,
President Obama had a dream, a dream that seemed impossible
                                        for him,
He believed in himself and fought for his dream,
Now that he has grasped it he will never let it go,
As he is a believer in dreams,
And he inspires me as he proved that dreams can come true,
But only if you fight for them and always have hope,
Because at this very moment he will be sitting at his resolute desk,
Making arrangements that he has always dreamed to do,
He is living his dream.

Abby Hare (11)
The King Edmund School

136

I Miss You

I tried to overcome my love for you
Overcome everything you put me through.
Every single thing I do
I can't help but think of you.
Every time I feel a tear
I lie in bed full of fear.
My love for you will always grow
Until the day I let you go
No matter what you do or say
My love for you will always stay
I know I love you
I feel it's true
So if you asked
I would say, 'I do.'

Connie Harrison (14)
The King Edmund School

Animals

I have a dream
That they will be in our team
No poaching for animals
In their breeding no falls
Even rats need respect
They are a mirror, they reflect
We will join as a team as we once did
In the cavemen times, when we hid
From the beautiful beasts
And had feasts
So we shouldn't kill
Should build them a home on a hill
We will live again
They shall have no pain.

Abigail Mallard (11)
The King Edmund School

Guns And Knives

There are people on the street,
Out there killing people.
If you get caught
You spend your life in prison
No job, no money, no life.

You think back to the old times
And think, *was it really worth it?*
When you're holding the knife
Ready to strike.
When really you should have thought twice.

You've taken a life,
But at the end of the day
You're going to be the one that has to sacrifice.

Sherele Lord (13)
The King Edmund School

Worldwide Insanity

Underage sex,
That's the mentality of kids today,
Gun and knife crime, it's not good
Too many gangstas bowling it down the streets
Thinking they own the place.

Bullying is vile, all bullies think they're perfect
But they're actually not
They hate themselves and what they are,
So they take it out on others,
They are a *disgrace*.

Terrorists threatening our towns and cities,
They deserve to die, killing the innocent,
What a bunch of wasters.

Connor Miles (13)
The King Edmund School

War

One calls him God
Another calls him Allah
One has the oil
Another wants it
One attacks
One defends
One has weapons
One has will
One seeks glory
One seeks normality
One is at war
Another is at war
Thousands die.

Thomas Bridge (13)
The King Edmund School

Don't Get Detentions

Don't get detentions 'coz they really, really suck
I think it's better eating dog's muck
Half hour or a whole sitting in class
I would rather walk on broken glass.

Ways you can get them is talking in class,
Or even messing about, throwing stuff
Forgetting to do homework, or not handing it in
But probably the worst, chewing gum.

If you're really naughty, you could get a Saturday detention
With Miss Stone, or even Miss Nichole
Sitting in a room all alone
So don't get detentions, OK!

Josh Walker (12)
The King Edmund School

The Poverty Heroes

Looking out across the plain-land
Everything is bare
The other people on this Earth
Do they truly care?

I'm hungry and I'm naked
My skin is raw and bare
My mother is ill and suffering
And you people still don't care.

My mother's slowly dying
I cry myself to sleep
I'm starving now
I don't know how you people can sleep at night.

Next day they start arriving
They helped me with my mum
I truly started to believe
I thought her time had come.

Things are looking better now
Our village is restored
These people they're my saviours
We all watch and applaud.

They're leaving now
They are moving on
But they've promised
They've assured
If ever I need any help
They'll come

My hope in other humans now has been fully restored.

Alice White (13)
The Sandon School

140

The Kind Man

He works with a charity
He is so kind to all the kids
All the boys and girls,
Who started life so bad.
But then he came along,
And now their life is better,
He has helped them so much.

He gives them a place to go,
A place that's warm and sae.
Somewhere out of trouble.
Somewhere to make friends.
They all look up to him,
He is their idol.

He helps them with anything,
From homework to big trouble.
He not only helps the kids
But their families as well.

So that's who inspires me,
He does all this,
All for free!

Eleanor Crussell (12)
The Sandon School

Poverty Poem

With no money to buy seeds
And no one to care
People keep dying
Do you think this is fair?

Homeless and hungry, starved to the bone
They have no money and have no home
Day by day thousands will die
No one to help them or hear them cry.

Many times this road has been walked
Why aren't we listening, why don't we talk?
How can we just ignore the lives that are lost
It's not happening to us who cares about the cost?

Wondering what lies ahead for the rest of the day
All they can do is hope and pray
That things will get better
And that everything will go their way.

Amy Hasler (13)
The Sandon School

My Inspiration Poem

What inspires me is not to be a catastrophe
I want to be a star like Bruce Lee
Or be as big as Ben Stiller
I could be a star in a thriller
Not something boring like guide touring
I'd rather watch bread thaw
I can fix a drawer
But I want to be something more
I want to be a famous man
Not putting baked beans in a tin can
What I really don't want to be
Is a catastrophe.

Rhys Emery (12)
The Sandon School

My Parents

My dad, my father, my light in the sky
My mum, my mother, my flower
Nothing will ever pass them by
As long as they have the power

To stand up for what they think is right
To stand up and speak up
But be polite
Their love comes in, cup by cup

My parents have done a lot for me
They are proud and happy of what I've done
Just like them, that's what I want to be
To me they are my bright yellow sun

There's nothing like a loving family

They've let me live forever happily.

Aimee Tompkins (13)
The Sandon School

Happiness

When the sun shines happiness makes me smile
Laughter makes me cry for happiness too
When I haven't seen someone for a while
I will be so happy when I see you.
Frosty winters will bring a smile to my face
The sounds of birds singing in a high tree
Happiness is when I see peace and grace
When the colours of autumn I can see.
If other people smile it makes me too
Happiness can be nearly anywhere
It can be my most things that you could do
Even by small things which you can share.
Happiness is loving and really good
So pass on the smile you really should.

Emma Till (13)
The Sandon School

My Special Bubble

Her golden-brown hair shines in the sunlight,
Her ears so tall, like a giant up high.
She would protect her friend if in a fight,
She may be super but she cannot fly.
When she is near I feel so very safe,
She makes me happy when I am so sad.
When she is with me I always have faith,
She would never make me angry or mad.
She always puts a smile onto my face,
When she jumps up high and turns in the sky.
She moves so very fast with lighting pace,
No cat could catch her, however they try.
My heart is so full, with love just for her,
What can I say, it's her golden-brown fur.

Alice Brookes (12)
The Sandon School

Steven Gerrard

Steven Gerrard his stature so immense,
He will pick out the illustrious pass.
He'll get you a goal when it's most tense.
Shooting and scoring he is just world class.
Out in Istanbul he won it five times.
In Germany he led us to 5-1.
The Liverpool fans sing out all his rhymes.
The FA cup he scored the goal, job done.
Against Arsenal he gifted Henry.
Recently he nearly moved to Chelsea,
That made all the Gooners very happy.
He didn't go because he was too wealthy.
So Stevie G is just pure quality,
But yet he is still not as good as me!

Harry Kindell-Brown (13)
The Sandon School

Samuel's Treasure

You put it with butter in sandwiches,
You can put it on toasted bread.
It was the treasure of Pepys Samuels,
As for it, he risked his head.
There is Edam, there is Babybel,
There is also Brie and whatever.
But Samuel Pepys risked a living hell,
For his lump of matured Cheddar.
It was the baker's bread that caught fire,
As if to prove that the cheese was great.
London's situation became dire.
And the cheese was kept alive by fate.
On that day five people are said to have died,
Plus the cheese that was buried alive.

James Moodey (13)
The Sandon School

Inspire

What really is inspiration?
What does it do for me or you?
Think, really it's a massive complication,
If you asked me, I wouldn't have a clue.
How do I write something inspirational
Do I have to dig deep into my heart?
Oh, but I guess Obama, he was sensational,
He did anything he could right from the start.
So maybe we should all get up and go,
Why don't you stay here, please stop running,
Yes is now our word, never to be no,
Stand tall, be brave and be cunning.
But then suddenly your life's a mess, your world's on fire,
Maybe you should open your eyes, go inspire.

Joanne Swann (13)
The Sandon School

145

My Mum

She's always there for me when I feel sad,
I know she's there with reassuring smiles,
She is always there when my life gets bad,
With her by my side I could go miles.
When life gets hard she helps me get through it,
Through wind and rain I know she will be there,
She helps me go on, she says I can't quit,
I know she loves me, I know that she cares.
When she is with me my life gets brighter,
She is my light at the end of the tunnel,
She makes me strong; she makes me a fighter,
She makes   me in the right place like a funnel.
Without my mum I don't know where I'd be,
She helps me carry on, she inspires me.

Rachel Goddard (12)
The Sandon School

Carlos Tevez

Carlos Tevez is class at scoring goals
He also plays great for Argentina.
The gaps he finds he will run through the holes
If he's annoyed he will become meaner.
He's got class talent and he's got class skills.
He can humiliate you when he wants,
And he's been tested for any bad pills.
His name is on his boots in special fonts.
He really likes to play right up the top.
Tevez prefers not to play at the back
On his head it looks like he's got a mop.
For ages his boss has not got the sack,
Overall I think that he is world class
And Tevez will pick a quality pass.

Ryan Mark Hart (13)
The Sandon School

I Have A Dream 2009 - Essex

Young Writers Information